5.99.

ParenT**alk**

Guide to the
First Six Weeks

D1639270

0340785446

The **ParenT**alk Guide to the First Six Weeks

Annette Briley and Tim Mungeam

Series Editor: Steve Chalke

Illustrated by John Byrne

Hodder & Stoughton
LONDON SYDNEY AUCKLAND

British Library Cataloguing in Publication Data
A record for this book is available from the British Library

ISBN 0 340 78544 6

Typeset by Avon Dataset Ltd, Bidford-on-Avon, Warks

Printed and bound in Great Britain by
Clays Ltd, St Ives plc

Hodder and Stoughton
A Division of Hodder Headline Ltd
338 Euston Road
London NW1 3BH

Contents

Acknowledgements

Our thanks to everyone who shared their stories with us: all the Mums in the playground at Aylesford Primary School; friends at St Margaret's, Addington; the midwives and new parents at Maidstone Hospital; and everyone in the Maternal and Fetal Research Unit at St Thomas's Hospital. Thanks, too, to Maggie Doherty, Andy and Debbie Woods, Steve and Viv Bateman, Helen Needham, Penny and Jamie Sertin, Sarah and Neil Altman, Caren and Neil Farrow, Debbie Dale, Tim and Hannah Jeffery and Jacqui and Peter White for their invaluable insights. But most of all, our thanks and love to Jack, Finn, Peter, Simon and Freya for watching endless videos and eating too many pizzas for tea (!), and to Gary and Charlotte for loving us and always believing in us.

Six Billion (Plus One)

'I can remember driving home at 5.30 a.m. and thinking how amazing the experience, just three hours earlier, had been. It made me think that this must happen every second of every day around the world – like lots of little lamps being lit in the night.'

Andy – Dad to Sam aged 3 months

According to the 1998 World Health Report, every day 365,000 babies are born somewhere on this planet. You may have thought *you've* had a busy 24 hours but, since this time yesterday, some 300,000 (ish) mothers have laboured, countless fathers have waited anxiously and 365,000 first breaths have been taken. Millions of friends and relatives have cooed at the first sight of a newborn baby.

And now it's *your* turn. It could be your first, second, third or fifteenth. But suddenly – especially if it's your first time around – the fact that a third of a million babies were born in the last 24 hours doesn't make a scrap of difference. Even the reality that a further 6 billion of us, already here, have all managed successfully to negotiate our own birth experience, matters not a jot. This time, it's all about *you* and preparing for *your* baby's birth. It's all about *your* labour and delivery. It's about *your* new role as a mum or a dad.

Few would argue that there is something truly wondrous about a new life. Regardless of the circumstances surrounding a baby's conception and arrival, when he or she actually appears in the world, everything seems to stop, just for a moment. Just for that second, the world seems a simpler place. Their sheer newness and tiny-ness – a little person, helpless and vulnerable – can catch even the hardest heart unawares.

But, as any parent will tell you (often incessantly!), from that point on, mum, dad and baby (and everyone else involved with this new life) begin a journey up a very steep learning curve. Every day brings with it fresh challenges, joys, tears, failures and successes, as you all get to grips with your new roles.

> **Top Tip:** Parenthood is an incredibly steep learning curve with every day bringing a new challenge – but it can still be great fun!

This book aims to help you prepare for, and then make the most of, the first six weeks of parenthood. This is undoubtedly the time when, for most of us, the enormity of the task ahead really begins to sink in. We have deliberately tried to make this book intensely practical, but our hope is that throughout its pages you will sense an undercurrent of celebration – a celebration of children, of parents and of the wider family.

'Wonder Woman, Superman and the Karate Kid All Live in Our House'

Professor Lesley Anne Page, in her book *The New Midwifery: Science and sensitivity in practice* (Churchill Livingstone, 2000), describes three mythological beings that many new parents are convinced can (and do) exist.

1. **Perfect Mother**
   Perfect Mother (alias 'Supermum') is that imaginary, glamorous creature who resembles the tissue or toilet soap

advertisements. Perfect Mother had a Perfect Birth and bonded with her Perfect Baby immediately, with no real need for change in her life. Her breasts never leaked, she could sit down immediately because she did not have an episiotomy and she certainly did not have breast engorgement. As for haemorrhoids and varicose veins – well what do you think? This perfect being immediately (before leaving the labour ward) went back to her pre-birth weight; her figure was once again 'to die for' and her stomach never ever stuck out.

Perfect Mother's hair and make-up are always flawless, her clothes stunning and her house immaculate. She never feels exhausted or fed up, or wishes that she had not had the baby, and she definitely, never, ever, ever stays in her dressing gown until lunchtime (or teatime). Her hair is always clean, her clothes are always tidy, her house is immaculate and she provides gourmet meals for her husband every night. Of course as well as all this she works full time outside the home.

2. **Perfect Father**
Perfect Father (or should we call him 'Superdad'?) also immediately adjusted to the birth of his children and became the perfect dad. He gazes adoringly at the Perfect Baby and Perfect Mother all of the time when he is not working at his perfect, stress-free job. He is, of course, such a help to 'Supermum' (not that she needs his help). And he never, ever loses his temper or shouts at his children. Oh, and of course he always looks perfect in his immaculately clean and ironed clothes (courtesy of the Perfect Mother).

3. **Perfect Child**
Within the idealistic, romanticised myth of parenthood, Perfect Baby gains exactly the right amount of weight every

week, never vomits, never, ever has colic, rarely cries, slept through the night from 1 week onwards and smiles at everyone all the time. In turn Perfect Child is always endearing, sweet, cooperative, quiet and loveable. Sweet, endearing Perfect Baby and Perfect Child do not require their parents to make any changes to their well-ordered existence, and they never, ever disrupt their lives.

Written in black and white and seen in the cold light of day, pictures like this cause a little chuckle. No one really thinks it's going to be like that, do they? But at the same time, in a world where we are bombarded with magazines, TV programmes, billboard adverts and other images depicting 'idyllic family life', it's easy to be conned. Before we know it, we are sucked into this idealised, stylised and sterilised view of family life and can feel twinges of disappointment when our own version doesn't seem to come up to scratch.

Top Tip: *Perfect Mum and Perfect Dad do not exist – the reality of parenthood is nothing like its Hollywood image.*

The truth is, most families are much more like TV's *The Royle Family* than we'd ever dare to admit. Even the designer couple with the designer baby who live down the road and seem to be keeping it all together will still have had to face their fair share of anxieties, failures and disappointments. They may well be different to yours, but they are issues just the same. Every parent faces problems as time goes by – always remember that what you see is only ever a small part of a much bigger picture. It's all just part of being human! Relax in the knowledge that Perfect Mother, Perfect Father and Perfect Child do not really exist – as one mum was heard to say, '*Real* parents wear dribble!'

As new parents, let's wear our dribble with pride (while, at the same time, making a mental note to buy more non-iron, non-'dry clean only' shirts at the earliest opportunity)!

 Top Tip: *Be prepared to make mistakes – even experienced parents still wear their parenting 'L-plates'! The important thing is to learn from any setbacks and move on.*

Parenting in a Nutshell

New parents are busy people. 'What did we do with all the spare time we used to have?' is a familiar cry. Once baby arrives, there's no time to read books – at least, not all the way through. So, if you're worried that you'll not even get the time to look at any of the other chapters in this book, here's the potted version:

Potted Principles for Prospective Parents

1. **Try to plan for what you can**
   There are things you can do to prepare yourselves emotionally, physically and practically for the arrival of your baby. Many of these will have been covered in conversations with your midwife or doctor. You will also have picked up ideas from your own parents, other relatives, friends and acquaintances – who either have, or are expecting, children. Parenting books and magazines can prove useful, too, in providing pointers about things to consider as you prepare for the big day. Talk things over with your partner, if you have one, or anyone else

who is going to have ongoing involvement in the birth and raising of your child.

2. **Try to relax about what you can't plan**
Do what you can to prepare yourself and your home for the new arrival, but don't expect to have every angle covered. No matter how many parenting books and magazines you read, parenthood will always be an ongoing learning experience! Even some of the things you're convinced you've got sewn up will undoubtedly come unravelled at some time or other!

Many parents remember visiting friends with children, long before they had any themselves, and thinking, 'We're certainly not going to raise our child like *that*!' Almost all of them recall discovering, years later, that they did exactly the same things they had judgementally disapproved of!

As he gets older, your baby's personality will emerge and that will dictate many of the ways in which you respond to him. At the moment, though, you haven't even met each other, so don't get too het up if you can't find the definitive solution for every parenting dilemma!

 Top Tip: Some things you can plan for and some you can't, so do what you can and relax about the rest.

---

3. **Appreciate the adjustment**
Looking after a baby is a major responsibility and an incredible challenge. It's no understatement to say that becoming a mum or dad totally transforms your life. Like it or not, things simply won't ever be the same again! There

will be things you previously took for granted that, temporarily at least, are no longer practicable. On the other hand, though, you'll be exposed to tremendous experiences as you get to know, and learn how to look after, your new baby.

People respond differently to this lifestyle change. For many first time mums and dads, coming to terms with this new role takes a bit of time. There are the inevitable feelings of inadequacy (Will I be a good enough parent?) coupled with 'bereavement' for the impending loss of independence. Both of these emotions are perfectly natural, so don't be too down on yourself if you experience them from time to time. Many parents admit that the thought of impending changes was nearly always much worse than the reality.

 Top Tip: Babies are life-changers, so prepare for the inevitable adjustments.

4. **Talk about it**
   It's vital to talk to other people about your feelings. It's vital, not just for you, but also for those around you (and that includes the baby). Who you decide to talk to depends, of course, on your own personal circumstances, but it could be:

   • Your partner
   • Your own parents, or your partner's
   • Friends with new babies
   • Friends with older children
   • Other trusted friends whom you respect
   • Your midwife, GP, health visitor, or practice nurse.

Waiting for the birth always brings with it an enormous mixture of emotions. Millions of things whizz around your mind as the baby's due date approaches – excitement and anticipation, hopes and dreams, fears and anxieties, funny little things that have happened during the latter stages of pregnancy and ideas for when the baby finally arrives.

People respond in different ways. Some are beside themselves with excitement and unable to wait for the big day to arrive. Others, however, may feel that their own parents didn't do a great job, and worry that they'll make the same mistakes. Dads often encounter feelings of 'What on earth have I done?' and 'What am I letting myself in for?'

All these emotions are perfectly natural, as long as they don't overwhelm you. And there is certainly no reason why they should prevent you from being a great mum or dad. That said, never let anything become a bigger issue than it should be by bottling it up. So give yourself an emotional check-up and don't be afraid to ask yourself some searching questions. You may find it helpful to write your thoughts down as you approach your baby's due date.

But always talk over your thoughts and concerns with your partner, and encourage them to tell you theirs. If you're on your own, choose someone to confide in whom you trust and who knows you well.

It sounds glib, but a problem shared often really *is* a problem halved. It's terribly 'un-British', of course, but having a chat with someone about an issue that's concerning you is a sure-fire way of feeling better. It might help put a different perspective on things, or prompt you to do something about your situation instead of just worrying about it. Alternatively, a timely, honest conversation may simply reassure you that there's nothing to worry about, or that you're not the only person who has ever felt the way you do.

Of course, you don't have to hop up onto the psychiatrist's couch every time you open your mouth – and the time to ask the question, '*Epidural – yes or no?*' probably *isn't* just as the FA Cup Final is about to kick off – but never shy away from talking to your partner or someone close about things that are important to you.

 Top Tip: *Talk to those around you – partner, friends, family – about how you feel about becoming a parent. It will make a big difference.*

5. **Share the load and enlist help**
New babies are hard work! Talk to your partner about how you intend dividing the tasks required to look after each other and your baby. If possible, agree to forget about the housework for a while (for those of us who *need* an excuse!), concentrating instead on the things that will allow you and your baby to keep healthy and rested.

Top Tip: *So long as it doesn't add to your stress, make a conscious decision to forget the housework for a while and concentrate on recovering from the birth and getting to know your new baby.*

It's also worth bearing in mind that you probably both have preconceived ideas about the tasks the other person will – and won't – do. This normally stems from the way that we ourselves were raised. For instance, did mum or dad do most of the nappy changing? Who cooked most of the meals? Who took the bin out when it was full? Talk about these things now, so that there is less chance of misunderstandings and tension when the time for action finally arrives. You don't have to set up a rota, but loosely agree between you how you intend to carve up the list of jobs – you can always swap things around at a later date if it's not working out.

Additionally, whenever possible in the early days, try to enlist the practical help of family and friends. That way you can conserve as much of your energy as possible to look after the baby. A cooked meal delivered to your door by a friend, when you feel you just can't face preparing anything, can make a world of difference. Accept offers of help with laundry, hoovering or washing-up graciously. Every little bit helps. Best of all, if you can arrange for 'helpers' to pop in for the occasional half-hour, you won't encroach on their time, and they won't outstay their welcome.

Don't be reluctant to accept offers of help – they'll normally come from people who know for themselves just what it's like to have a new baby to care for. You may decide to make your own list of people whom you can ask. If you present too much of an 'I've got it all together' image, they may be less keen to offer help in the future – just when you feel you could really use it.

One word of warning: always remember that this is *your* home and *your* baby. If you feel that you're being overwhelmed by visitors, however well-meaning, don't be afraid to regain control. The point of enlisting help is, after all, to *help* you, not to bring you extra pressure. The early weeks of parenthood are very special but also very fleeting and it's important that you and your partner feel that you've had ample opportunity to get to know the newest addition to your family. Remember, *you're* the parent now!

> *Top Tip: Graciously accept all offers of help –
> you'll need plenty to get through those early days
> – but always make sure that visitors ease your
> stress rather than add to it!*

6. **Remember it's tough at first, but it's worth it!**
Ed Asner once famously described parenthood as 'part joy,
part guerrilla warfare' and this is certainly true of the first
six weeks. It can feel as though you're living on your wits,
uncertain about the mission that lies ahead of you, and
with only the most meagre energy rations at your disposal.
But every day successfully negotiated, even taking into
account the inevitable setbacks, will mark a little rise in
your confidence and your ability to deal with tomorrow's
challenges.

You may be familiar with the following, often quoted,
statistics:

We retain:

- **10%** of what we **read**
- **20%** of what we **hear**
- **30%** of what we **see**
- **50%** of what we **watch demonstrated**
- **70%** of what we **discuss with others**
- **90%** of what we **'do'**

And the point? Simply that the only way to get the best
out of 'new' parenthood is to just get stuck in and learn on
the job. This is how humans learn best. And only once
you have immersed yourself in the hard work of nappy
changing, feeding, cuddling, walking, rocking, waking,

cooking and washing and 101 other things, can you ever fully appreciate the best bit about being a parent. This will be the time when you're fussing around – probably doing something incredibly practical, menial and boring – only to see your baby looking at you for the first time. And not just looking at you, but really *looking* at you, making contact – *connecting*. That will be when you genuinely realise that this really is all worth it!

 Top Tip: *Every parent learns 'on the job', so grab the bull by the horns and get stuck in!*

7. **You'll never be a perfect parent, but you can be a great one**
    Perfect Mother, Perfect Father and Perfect Child *do not exist*. The sooner that you come to terms with this, the freer you will feel to develop into the parent that you know you can be. Even parents of children who have long grown up and left home admit that they're still learning. It's not surprising really – none of our children came with a user manual (or instructions in eight languages!). As a parent you are on a stage with no script and no prior rehearsals; not even the most critical audience will expect a perfectly delivered performance.

    Appreciating our learner status helps in so many ways. It means we're less intimidated by other parents and the way they do things; we're more prepared to ask for advice and opinions from other, more experienced, parents; and we're less prone to beat ourselves up over every minor failure or setback.

    On the other hand, even though attaining perfection as a parent is beyond all of us, you can be a *great* parent – one that your child is proud of. As you'll see from the pages that follow, it takes time, hard work and a lot of persistence, but if you're prepared to put in the effort, it can be the most rewarding and worthwhile task in the world.

Top Tip: *Give yourself a break: you may not be perfect but you can be a truly successful parent, loved by your child.*

8. **Enjoy it!**
Thousands of men and women become parents every day and find that, not only can they be great parents, they can also love it too! OK, so none of us want to become 'baby bores' but, at the same time, don't we secretly envy someone who is so completely in love with their child that they cannot help but talk about them?

So whether you're a new or expectant mum, or dad, the message is the same. Get stuck in and enjoy the first six weeks! You'll never have it all sewn up, but you can do your best and savour the privilege of getting to know the newest member of the family.

Top Tip: *Becoming a parent is an incredible privilege but the time will fly by. Be determined to make the most of it now and enjoy it!*

How to Read This Book

Well the first bit of good news is that you don't have to read it – certainly not all of it anyway – from cover to cover. It has been deliberately split into 'common sense' sections which, we hope, will mean it's easy to dip in and out of. Pick the bits you want to read about and forget about the rest (at least until you need it).

It's also worth bearing in mind that *The First Six Weeks* is not intended to be an exhaustive manual – if you're after lengthy definitions and explanations of medical terminology, charts, diagrams and statistics, you're looking in the wrong place! What this book does do, however, is try to provide a bit of reassurance, practical advice and combined experience to help you chart your way through the seas of brand new parenthood. In order to avoid the unwieldy nature of constantly writing in all-inclusive language, throughout the book we have referred to babies only in the male gender ('he'). We hope that all the little girl babies (and their parents) will forgive us!

Here they are, then – hundreds of top tips and handy hints for making the most of the first six weeks. You can be sure that the next two months are going to be a rollercoaster ride – a mixture of exhilaration and fear – but, at the end of it all, our hope is that you'll be glad that you decided to jump on and enjoy the ride! So fasten your seatbelts!

Great Expectations

Getting Ready for the Big Arrival

Getting Ready Emotionally and Physically

I Get So Emotional Baby . . .

Towards the end of pregnancy and during the first few weeks
as parents you will both experience an incredible range of
emotions. It's perfectly normal to find yourself, as a mum or
dad, worrying whether you'll be 'good enough' as a parent.
For many people, the experience of approaching parenthood
may also stir up issues – good and not so good – about how
they themselves were raised. It's vital for you to be able to talk
to someone about these feelings, but also to recognise that
everyone goes through it to some extent.

There's no getting away from the fact that your life will
change completely. Even if you have had lots of contact with
small children you are both bound to feel an enormous
responsibility once your own child is born. And, of course, it

17

won't be just your life that changes – your parents may well be worrying about their role as grandparents, your brothers and sisters about theirs as aunts and uncles.

In the same way, many parents of one child are concerned about whether they could possibly love a second child as much as the first. Rest assured, you will discover another 'pot' of love, just as big, for your second child.

 Top Tip: *It's only natural to be a bit anxious about whether you'll be a good enough parent. Talk to others and listen to the advice of more experienced parents.*

Twenty-Four Seven

Many new mums and dads can't believe how much spare time they used to have B.C. ('Before Children'). Certainly, in the first few weeks parents often find themselves unprepared for the sheer time and energy that such a little person, who doesn't move around much and sleeps most of the day, can demand.

 Top Tip: *Newborn babies are very demanding – be realistic about what you will and will not be able to take on in the early days.*

So the trick here is to plan for what you can and be laid back about what you can't. A useful device sometimes employed by antenatal teachers is to draw a clock face with 24 hours on it. This represents your average day.

On the clock, map out your day – shade in areas to represent the main things you do, when you do them and the time it takes to get them done. Add the things that you have to do for everyday life (even though you may not want to) – food shopping, cleaning, laundry, etc. Add the things that you don't have to do, but enjoy doing occasionally (e.g. going out with friends, visiting the gym, reading, listening to music, watching TV and so on).

'Pre-Baby' Lifestyle

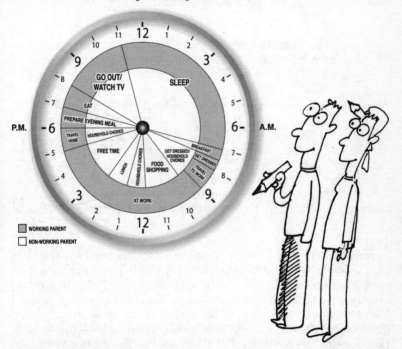

Take a look at what you've drawn and think about the things that, once the baby has arrived, you need, or would like, to be able to continue doing. Talk to your partner about what they are and why they are important.

Then comes the tricky bit. Add the baby's likely demands for the same 24-hour period to your clock face (see typical example below).

Baby's Daily Pattern

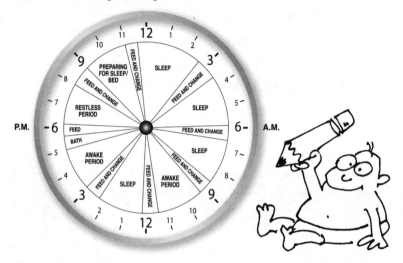

How do they fit in with your own expectations for the time that's going to be available to you. Will it work? Are you expecting too much, either of yourself or your baby? It's by no means an exact science, but many expectant mums and dads find the clock face idea to be useful as an indicator, helping them think through these 'time' issues. Your clock might help you decide, for example, that there are things you need to drop, albeit temporarily, to enable you to meet your baby's needs and ensure that you're looking after yourself. It may help you to identify times when you could ask friends and relatives to help out a bit in the early days (mealtimes, washing, cleaning etc.). The important thing is to talk to your partner/friends/ family about it and come to some understanding about what is and isn't important to you. Now is a good chance to do it – you'll have much less time later on.

Give Yourself a Break

During pregnancy, a woman's body is constantly working hard, so – as an expectant mum – it's important to rest as much as you can. Try to rest completely as well as doing things that you find relaxing (walking, swimming, talking to someone, listening to music or reading a good book). For men too, it's important to ensure that you're not exhausted before your partner goes into labour – when it happens, you'll want to support her as best you can and make the most of the moment, so try to take things a bit easier beforehand if you possibly can.

Once the baby arrives, the time you have to spend together, as a couple, will reduce significantly. Therefore, before baby's birth, try to ensure that you spend plenty of time together. Don't just sit around and 'veg out' – seek out relaxing activities that you both enjoy and share them together, making the most of one another's company.

Sex may be an important part of this for many couples (although, for others, it's the last thing on their mind!). Unless you have been advised by your doctor or midwife not to have sexual intercourse for medical reasons, it is perfectly safe during pregnancy, although you may need to be a bit more adventurous in finding comfortable positions for you both! In fact, sexual intercourse around the baby's due date, can be an effective way of making labour start! It might not be 100 per cent foolproof (nowhere near, in fact), but you can certainly have fun finding out whether it works for you!

> **Top Tip:** Set aside some time to spend with your partner before the baby comes. Once he arrives, your baby will be the focus of nearly all your attention – at least for a while, anyway!

Getting Ready ... Birth Plans

If you haven't written one already, your midwife may suggest that you consider writing a 'birth plan'. This is just a piece of paper, on which mums-(and dads-)to-be have written their thoughts about:

- Who the birth partner is going to be – this is the person who will accompany mum through her labour (usually, but not exclusively, the baby's father)
- Whether there is a particular midwife who you would, *ideally*, like to be present
- Positions for labour and delivery etc.
- Pain relief
- Monitoring
- How you feel about assisted deliveries (ventouse and forceps)
- How you feel about Caesarean section
- How you feel about an episiotomy (cut), or tearing
- Whether you want your baby handed straight to you, or cleaned up first
- Receiving Syntometrine (injection given to the mum to help speed up delivery of the placenta and control bleeding)
- Planned method of feeding (breast or bottle)
- Vitamin K for the baby
- If you would feel strongly about the presence of medical/midwifery students, as witnesses or clinicians
- How long you would, ideally, like to stay in hospital
- Any other things that you feel strongly about

Birth plans are useful because they help expectant parents think through some of the key issues surrounding the birth before they are faced with them in the labour ward. It would be a mistake, however, to view them as a ticket to the perfect labour – they aren't. While it's good to plan for most eventualities, you cannot be certain that things will go according to plan. Contrary to popular myth, and however much we would like our birth plans to dictate how things will actually go, childbirth is not an exact science – it is a natural process driven by the woman's body and, recent research suggests, by the baby itself.

Additionally, midwives and doctors have to make decisions

on the clinical evidence presented to them and the resources at their disposal, at any one time. For example, you may have written on your birth plan that you would prefer a water birth, only to discover on the day that someone is already using it, or your baby needs monitoring more closely than is possible when a woman labours or delivers in the water. Because your health and the wellbeing of your baby are of paramount importance to all the midwives and doctors looking after you, a birth plan is useful for them. It tells them where you are coming from and how you would, ideally, like things to go. But labour is an uncharted journey, and you cannot plan for everything, so be prepared to be flexible.

Top Tip: *Birth plans help you think through your preferences for the birth and, at the very least, the things you* don't want. *But be flexible – childbirth is not an exact science!*

If, during labour, things begin to go very differently from the way you want them to, most midwives will try to explain why at the time. If, however, they have had to work quickly, with no time for explanation, they will come back and talk to you afterwards. (By the way – and because nearly everyone asks – those who opt for a Caesarean section *cannot* have liposuction at the same time!)

Getting Ready . . . Birth Partners

Think about who is going to be present at the actual birth. For most people, but not exclusively, it is the father of the baby. The 'Dads of Old' who left their labouring wives at the door of the delivery suite, and headed off for the pub, are almost a thing of the past! Most men want to be as involved as possible in the birth itself.

Agreeing to be present during labour, however, is not always as straightforward a decision as it may sound. Many men feel under pressure to be at the birth – not necessarily from their partners or the doctors and midwives – but from work colleagues, family and friends. An almost audible sharp intake of breath accompanies even the mention of the possibility that a dad might choose not to be at the birth.

If, however, as the father of the baby, you really do not want to be present, or have reservations about it, talk to your partner and the midwives and doctors who are caring for you. Most men agree that, although they didn't relish the prospect, they are actually overwhelmed with emotion once the baby is finally delivered and look back on it as a truly wonderful experience. Some men, on the other hand, feel they can handle a 'normal' birth, but would not want to be present at a Caesarean birth.

> **Top Tip:** *It's perfectly natural for men to be anxious about the labour. Talk to your partner about how you feel.*

If you're unsure whether, when it comes down to it, you'll be able to be present throughout, have a good friend or relative in reserve, with whom your partner feels totally comfortable and who can step in to be alongside her if necessary. In most maternity units, even if he hasn't been present at the birth, dad can still be very nearby and see the baby immediately after delivery. If you are unsure, tell the midwife caring for your partner during labour. Men aren't forced to remain in the room throughout, and many find they can manage small chunks, interspersed with walks around the car park! You are free to come and go as you please, just remember the number of the room your partner is in, for your return!

IF I'M PRESENT AT THE BIRTH, CAN I HAVE TIME OFF DURING THE OBNOXIOUS TEENAGE YEARS?

Getting Ready . . . Packing 'The Bag'

Your midwife will have told you about packing a bag to take into hospital with you. This still holds true even if you are planning to have a home birth, just in case you need to be taken into hospital for any reason at short notice. During your pregnancy your midwife should have given you an indication of the basic contents that should go into your bag – which can vary slightly, depending on which hospital you are going to – but a few extra things worth considering are:

1. **When you're packing the bag, remember to think about the needs of the birth partner as well as mum**
   Dads and other birth partners pass out at delivery for three main reasons:

   i) *They are too hot.* Labour wards are always incredibly hot, so wear a T-shirt under your sweatshirt, so you can peel off a layer! Some people wear shorts too, (but you can feel a little daft leaving the maternity unit on a cold December night!).
   ii) *They are hungry.* Make sure you pack plenty of 'munchies', to get you through labour! Partners can usually use hospital canteens, but are rarely offered food on the maternity unit. Most partners are offered the odd cup of tea or coffee during the labour, but you might find you need extra fluid. Put in a few extra 'tinnies' (of soft drinks, not beer!).
   iii) *They are tired.* It can be totally exhausting, mentally and physically, especially if you have been working all day, to head for the labour ward in the evening. You can end up going for more than 24 hours without sleep. Doze when you can and sit down, rather than pace the floor!

2. **Take a list of the phone numbers of all the people you need to ring once the baby arrives**
You'll want to tell everyone about the baby, so make sure you'll have their phone numbers to hand. Also think about the order in which you're going to ring everyone – get this one wrong and you are in *serious* trouble!

3. **Make sure you've got enough change for pay phones and car parks**
Mobile phones must be switched off in hospitals, as they affect bleep systems and other important equipment, so a payphone may be the next best option (especially if the new mum herself wants a word!). Start collecting change now – you'll be amazed at how much money a quick look between and behind the sofa cushions, under the bed and in all your trouser pockets can produce! Many hospitals also have 'pay and display' car parks and you're likely to want to park there for some time. A useful tip worth remembering is that many hospitals only expect you to pay once a day for parking and will 'exempt' you from paying again whilst accompanying someone in labour, even if you have to park more than once.

4. **Pack a camera, and spare film**
If you have a very valuable or complicated camera, you may find a 'single use' camera is a good investment – it's easier to use and there's less worry about losing it. Remember to get the indoor type with a flash. Keep it close at hand because babies pull wonderful facial expressions in the early days! Video cameras can be used in hospitals, but few units will allow you to video the delivery (who would you show it to anyway?!). Remember to get the consent of any member of staff you want to film.

5. **Pack clothes to return home in**
   You probably won't want to put maternity clothes back on, so something bigger than usual – baggy but comfortable – is usually good. Think about what you'd like to wear – it'll help you feel better about yourself if, despite being knackered, you're confident that you look OK. And don't forget your shoes – you'd be surprised how many women go home in their slippers! Or their partner's coat!

6. **Pack your oldest knickers to use after your baby is born (women only, not men!)**
   You can throw them away if they get stained and the elastic is usually a bit more lax, so they won't dig into you. This is useful because, unfortunately, you are unlikely to regain your sylph-like figure immediately after delivery!

   Avoid paper knickers – they aren't terribly effective! Most hospitals cover everything in plastic, and are usually very warm, so you will be hot, and the paper fabric used in these pants tends to shred! The narrow elastic also tends to be quite tight, and can dig in as you move around. If you are really unlucky you can end up with completely shredded pants and a tight piece of elastic around your middle! Not great for boosting your self-image!

   If you have had a Caesarean section you will also need knickers which are *big*! You will hate them, but 'granny-style' pants that come well above your scar (which will be below your bikini line) really are the most comfortable. Send a sympathetic friend or relative down to the nearest market to buy the cheapest ones possible, and make them promise not to laugh (or tell anyone else!).

Top Tip: *Think carefully about what to pack in your hospital bag. Avoid taking everything but the kitchen sink with you, but have spare items at home that can be brought in if necessary.*

Getting Ready . . . The Right Equipment

Even the briefest of strolls down any high street alerts you to just how many things you can buy for you and your baby. Every gadget and gizmo promises to be the 'must have', which – once you own it – you'll always wonder how you ever did without. Unfortunately it's also easy to read more of an underlying message into such advertising – that, should you decide *not* to buy, you'll somehow be seen as a *lesser* parent, because you're not putting your baby's best interests first. Will you scar him forever? Will he be emotionally traumatised due to the constant bumping around in his bargain pushchair – just because *you* were too *mean* to invest in the latest three-wheeled, 'off-road' Supercomfort ZX3000 buggy, with gears? Will he ever forgive you? Oh, the guilt!

Undoubtedly, there have been some great innovations over the past few years and some of them will, of course, prove invaluable. But as you get ready, here are some things to bear in mind:

- *Do not be tempted to go out and buy one of everything you* **might** *need for baby.* Despite all the advertising campaigns, no one needs *absolutely* everything! Think about your lifestyle. For example, do you really need to invest in an expensive pram? Will you use it? Do you use public transport or a car? Is the pram easy to fold and carry? Does it fit into the boot of your car?

- *Do not buy loads of first-size clothes.* All new babies grow rapidly, and you will be surprised how many clothes you will receive as presents once baby is born. And don't rip the labels off everything you are given – you may want to exchange some for bigger sizes.
- *Beg, steal and borrow equipment!* Many people keep old baby clothes and bits of equipment, just in case. Quite probably, although these things are 'old' to them, in actual fact they are almost brand new (especially baby clothes which are grown out of almost as soon as they are worn!). Ask around amongst your own family and friends to see if they have suitable things that you could borrow. And once you get on the new parent circuit – borrowing and lending clothes and equipment – you'll be amazed at the savings you can make, and still have the best-dressed baby on the street!

31

If you borrow or buy second-hand equipment, always make sure it has been well maintained and is safe (with appropriate safety marks, like the CE mark).

The National Childbirth Trust (NCT) often have second-hand sales – check the noticeboards in your local antenatal clinic, local shops and halls as well as your local newspaper. There are often bargains to be had!

 Top Tip: Don't be tempted to buy one of absolutely everything *you might need for a 21st century baby! Instead, work out what you need for your lifestyle.*

Buggies and Prams

If you can't borrow someone else's, buying a pram or buggy (even second-hand) can be a major investment for new parents. It's good to take a bit of time to think about what you're after before hitting the shops:

- Decide what your budget is and agree not to exceed it.
- Try as many different types of pram as you can, before you buy.
- Make sure it fits in the boot of your car (especially if it's a double buggy).
- Ensure the pram meets all your requirements. If you are using it from birth, make sure it lies completely flat, but will convert to the sitting-up type for when your child is a bit older. And remember you will undoubtedly be taking your baby out in the rain on many occasions so make sure the pram has an adequate rain cover. It's also worth checking that the water doesn't just pour off the covers all over your feet when you are pushing baby around in the rain!

- Think about the overall size of the pram you are buying. Remember doorways and shop aisles tend to be narrow, as do some footpaths. Also think about getting the pram in and out of your home, through doors and gates.
- Make sure the buggy you choose is comfortable for your height and your stride. If possible, try to get one that is adjustable in terms of handle height – especially if you and your partner differ in height by several inches. If you are tall, you don't want to get backache in the first five minutes (a baby and a buggy together weigh more than you might think!). Similarly, make sure that your natural stride doesn't mean that you are forever clipping the back of the buggy with your toes – it gets very annoying after a while!
- If you do borrow a buggy or buy a second-hand one, make sure that it carries the appropriate safety marks and is in good condition (preferably having been recently serviced by a reputable dealer).

 Top Tip: *For all larger equipment purchases, always shop around and try before you buy. If you borrow any equipment, make sure it is in good condition, carrying the proper safety marks.*

Car Seats
These are worth a special mention because it is a legal requirement in the UK to ensure that all passengers in a car are secured using a seat appropriate for their height and weight. If you intend taking your baby home from hospital by car you must have a car seat for the journey and if you regularly travel by car you *must* invest in one.

- Make a list of your requirements and talk to other people, who have had a baby, about the pros and cons of their choice.
- There are numerous models available, so don't be afraid to go to local shops, and try them out. Speak to the shop assistants, who should be able to advise you further.
- Remember the weight they state on the box *excludes* the baby!
- Car seats come with a variety of different handles, so try holding a few to see which is the most comfortable. Since the advent of car seats several GPs and other healthcare professionals have suggested that some adults develop shoulder problems, which may be associated with carrying children for long periods of time in car seats. For this reason, if at all possible, you should avoid standing holding a baby in his car seat. But because it will be unavoidable sometimes, it is vital that you're as comfortable as possible.
- Some pram systems have a first car seat attachment, but think very carefully as to whether it is cost effective for you to invest in one of these.
- Remember that some rear facing car seats are not suitable for use in cars with passenger seat airbags.
- Once you've made your choice, make sure you know exactly how your seat actually works! Ensure that you're familiar with the way the straps fit properly around the baby, but also how the seat is fitted in the car. Recent studies by manufacturers have discovered that a large proportion of people know neither how to properly secure the car seat in a car, nor a child in the seat. In fact, you would be amazed just how many people spend quite a lot of time standing in the hospital car park, getting very frustrated, trying to secure their baby seat for the first time!
- Remember you will need to adjust the straps that secure the baby, not only as he grows, but also depending on the clothes he is wearing.

> **Top Tip:** *It is a legal requirement to strap your child into an appropriate car seat whenever he travels in a car. Remember the weight on the box excludes the weight of the baby and that new babies grow fast!*

Getting Ready for Feeding and Changing

These two activities are going to take up a lot of your time in the first weeks, so it's worth thinking about ways that you can make things easier on yourself:

- *If you intend to breastfeed your baby, only be measured for one or two nursing bras.* Your shape, and size, will change on an almost daily basis during the first week after giving birth, and it is far better to be re-measured once you have had baby. If, after the birth, the size remains comfortable, you can always keep the box and send someone back to the shop for another identical one.

  One mum, having had a Caesarean section, was visited by a male friend who was also visiting to see someone else in another part of the hospital. He was heading into town to get some bits and pieces for this other patient, and called in to ask if she needed anything. She handed him the box her nursing bra came in and said, 'I need another one, just like this'. He duly returned with exactly the right thing, totally convinced that she was only testing their friendship!

- *If you intend to bottle-feed your baby, try to avoid the temptation to go out and buy half a dozen identical bottles and teats.* Some infants can be very fussy and you may find that you have to try quite a few before you discover which suit your child best.

- *Many mums find washable breast pads very useful.* They are soft and comfortable, very absorbent, easy to wash and dry quickly. They are environmentally friendly, and cost effective. However do not iron them! They stick to the iron and you have to peel them off, after which they are never quite the same again!

  There are two types of disposable breast pads. The first is the cheaper flat pad, but these tend to shred when wet, and may, occasionally, leave you feeling damp and uncomfortable. The second type is a shaped pad which is generally more reliable. These pads are expensive though and if you tend to 'leak' (and some women do more than others) you will need lots and the cost can soon add up. Avoid buying hundreds of one kind of breast pad – in practice, you may find one type suits you better than another.

- *Many new parents seem to find that cheap, small nappies (particularly supermarket 'own brand' ones) work really well for small babies.* They absorb moisture well, and also provide a snug fit for both boys and girls (thus preventing leaks). In a straw poll amongst new mums and dads for the purposes of this book, all said that they would advise new parents to buy the cheapest nappies available for the first few weeks when changing is most frequent. When your baby is older, and needs changing less frequently, it can pay to buy the more expensive, super-duper 'stay-dry lining' type.

- *Cotton wool rolls are better value than balls for babies' tender little places.* The woolly balls also tend to be too small for cleaning a really dirty bottom. If you buy the cotton wool rolls you can tear off a large piece, if required. If you would rather have ready-made cotton balls, again buy the roll and make your own, whilst watching TV! (Older children can be good at doing this!)

Top Tip: *Wait a while before buying bumper packs of things like nappies and breast pads. You might have to try out a few before discovering what works best for you and your baby.*

The New Baby Checklist

A quick run down of the basics to have at, or soon after, the birth:

- 6 x newborn vests ❑
- 6 x newborn Babygros ❑
- Cardigans ❑
- Scratch mitts (although most newborn Babygros have ❑ 'hatches' for hands, which stay in place better than scratch mitts)
- Cellular blankets depending on time of year ❑
- Outdoor clothing/blankets/hats ❑
- Cot or 'Moses' basket and bed linen ❑
- Sterilising equipment ❑
- Infant formula (if relevant) ❑
- 3 x bottles and newborn teats (if relevant) ❑
- 1 pack of muslin squares ❑
- Breast pads ❑
- 2 x nursing bras ❑
- Big knickers for mum ❑
- Maternity pads ❑
- 1 large pack of newborn nappies ❑
- Nappy sacks, or a supply of plastic bags ❑
- Baby wipes ❑
- Changing mat ❑
- Barrier cream for nappy rash (if not using nappies ❑ with stay dry lining)
- Cotton wool rolls ❑
- Unperfumed babybath suitable for washing body and ❑ hair
- 1 x baby sponge (with cut-out baby shape) ❑
- 1 x large soft towel ❑
- Baby hairbrush/comb ❑
- Nightlight for night-time changing and feeds (or ❑ low wattage bulb for bedside lamp)
- Buggy, pram, or baby sling ❑

- Baby intercom ☐
- Car seat ☐
- 1 (or more) x baby! ☐

Plus friends/family on hand to get you other things once you discover (if you do!) that you need them.

Getting Ready Financially

'What a dear little thing!' exclaimed the proud grandmother. 'Too right!' muttered the new dad, under his breath! How right they both were! Children are not cheap – for many of us, if we waited until we could afford one, we'd never do it! Of course, as you get yourself ready for the baby's arrival, the last thing you will want to dominate your thinking is money but, as they say, 'a stitch in time saves nine', so it's wise to pay some attention now to the 'F' question – finance.

Top Tip: It may not be at the top of your list of priorities, but any time getting your financial affairs in order will be time well spent.

Think about:

- *General financial planning.* It's reckoned that, in the first year of their baby's life, a parent spends about £300 on nappies alone, never mind all the other essentials your new baby will require! With all this new pressure on your wallet, having a new baby is a very common time for parents to get into serious debt, so it's a wise move to try and get on top of your financial situation before it's put under added strain.

Make a list of your monthly income and set against it your regular monthly outgoings. Then add to your 'spending' list the amount of money you think you spend on other things such as food, petrol, clothes, going out, etc. If you have less money coming in than going out, it's time to take a hard look at how you're going to make ends meet. You may need to curb your spending a little – setting targets for how much you can spend per week or month can often help.

If you're buying baby equipment keep an eye on how much you're spending – it's easy for large costs to soon mount up before the baby's even arrived. Be wary of building up large credit card bills that you may have difficulty paying back later.

If you're on a low income, you may be eligible to receive a Sure Start Maternity Grant (for up to £300) to help with the extra costs that come with a new baby. You can pick up a form or get further information about this from your local Social Security Office.

Top Tip: *Babies are not cheap, so try to pay off as many debts as you can before the baby arrives. Avoid accumulating additional loans that you may have difficulty paying back later.*

- *Maternity pay rights and leave arrangements.* If you have been employed and are taking maternity leave, it's important to know what income you can expect during this time as well as the details of when you are expected to return to work (should you decide to go back). Even if you intend returning to work there is often a shortfall in income whilst you are on maternity leave and checking this out now will avoid the stress of doing it later with a baby on your arm! Most employers require you to inform them about your intentions with regard to your maternity leave and returning to work. Talk things through with your boss or personnel department and find out your rights and entitlements. This will save a lot of stress at a later date.

- *Paternity leave.* More and more employers are beginning to provide paid paternity leave and it is likely to become a statutory requirement in the not too distant future. If you work, talk to your partner about how to make the most of any paternity leave that you may have. Even if you work for a small company most employers will allow a dad a day off for the birth of their baby. Again, tell your employers when baby is due, and negotiate time off in advance. If, even in these more enlightened times, your employer insists that any paternity leave will be unpaid, you will need to take this into account in your financial planning.

Top Tip: *Make sure you fully understand your maternity and paternity rights.*

- *Making a will.* Morbid maybe, but making a will ensures that your child, on your death, will inherit everything that you want them to with the minimum of red tape and fuss. For lots of people the making of a will coincides with the birth of their first child. There are a number of companies who specialise in wills and they don't have to cost a lot of money. Once you have children, part of the will-making process will involve appointing a guardian (or guardians) for your child. The person helping you to draw up your will should explain at length what this entails, but it's never too early to think about the people you would like to invite to take on this important responsibility.

Top Preparation Tips for Mums and Dads

A lady on a postnatal ward really thought she'd got everything covered. She had just had their second child, and remembered how upset she had felt when her partner had not brought her flowers and fruit the first time round. This time she was not going to feel left out! Before going into labour, she filled the fruit bowl at home with lots of different fruits, and having given birth and been transferred to the postnatal ward, she told her husband to bring the fruit in with him next time he visited. Imagine her surprise when he walked into the ward clutching their three-year-old's hand, but otherwise with no packages.

'Where's the fruit?' she hissed under her breath. She was amazed when he produced an apple and an orange from his pockets. He then explained the rest was at home, because he thought she wanted him to bring in some every day!

You can't be prepared for every eventuality, but there are some things you can do now to make life easier following the birth of your baby. If you are very organised, or your baby is late, you may like to occupy yourself by doing some of the following in readiness for the new arrival. If you are superstitious, however, and would rather not get too much done prior to the 'big day', these might be the sort of things a loyal partner, family member or friends could do prior to mum and baby coming home.

As D-day approaches:

- Stock up on things like toilet rolls, washing powder and nappies.
- Fill cupboards with pasta, tinned foods, cereals etc. – foods with long 'sell by' dates.
- Fill the freezer with food.
- Make extra portions in the last weeks of pregnancy and freeze them. Label them first, unless you really don't mind a complete surprise for dinner.
- Make address labels (on a computer or by hand) or label envelopes ready for baby announcement cards.
- Make a list of everyone who offers to help (and their phone numbers!). People like to be needed and will be only too pleased to help in whatever way they can. The trouble is, it's very easy to forget who said they could help and when! You may also want to take this opportunity to set up a few hot meal 'deliveries' for the first couple of days after you all return home, or for dad while he's popping backwards and forwards to the hospital.

Top Tip: Get yourself as organised as possible before the birth. Do it now, while you've got the chance!

'And Here's One
We Made Earlier . . .'

Immediately After the Birth

As a brand new mum, you will need to allow yourself time to recover from labour and delivery, as even the most straightforward of births can leave you feeling shell shocked. Labour is very appropriately named – it is probably the hardest day's work you'll ever do in your life! The funny thing is that though you can feel absolutely exhausted towards the end of labour, immediately your baby has been born, you can feel full of energy again. Unfortunately, this state cannot last for too long, so try not to do too much!

Dads, too, can find labour physically and mentally exhausting. They are often amazed at the energy their partners exhibit immediately after the baby is born and, at this point, are probably even more tired than mum! Although mum will normally assume the role and responsibility of main carer in the first day or so, dad can often find himself racing around, ringing friends and family and generally going to and fro between hospital and home. Even with a home birth, the same can be true – chores to be done, shopping to be bought, visitors to be coordinated. Wanting to get things sorted out is only natural, but it's important that you give yourself a bit of time, immediately after the birth, just to recover and rest, happy in the knowledge that you're a new parent.

 Top Tip: *Everyone takes a while to recover from the birth and adjust to their new roles, so give yourself a bit of time.*

Getting Used to Parenthood

Regardless of whether they have had a hospital or a home birth, during the early postnatal period, many women experience a huge range of feelings. These may include excitement, trepidation, happiness, love, fear, pain, discomfort and many more! It's perfectly natural to feel as though you're on an emotional rollercoaster!

Many men find this a difficult time, as they see their normally even-tempered partner swing from one extreme mood to another. It can be hard for them to anticipate how to react – what to say and when (and when not to say anything at all!). New fathers, too, experience many emotions. Apart from the tiredness that invariably results from supporting their partner and witnessing the birth, there's the mixture of elation and trepidation that comes with the earliest hours of fatherhood. Many men feel they now have more responsibility than ever before.

Top Tip: *Be prepared for the emotional roller-coaster that sends your feelings all over the place.*

'Well, What Were You Expecting?'

Not all parents catch a first glimpse of their brand new, wrinkly, red baby and instantly adore him. Looking back, many mums and dads confess that the baby was not quite what they expected, and the same may happen to you. It could be that:

- You secretly thought (and even hoped) that he would be a girl (or vice versa).
- You're shocked by how he looks.
- You were hoping that he'd have lots of hair, but he hasn't.
- You're disappointed that he doesn't look more like you.

New mums and dads are often racked with guilt as they experience these feelings for themselves, not realising that, to a certain extent, it's pretty normal. Building a relationship with anyone takes time, but especially with someone who has yet to fully develop ways of communicating with you. So give yourself a break – the vast majority of mums and dads find their love for their baby grows as their relationship with him develops. The pace at which this occurs can vary tremendously, but eventually you'll look back and wonder how you ever got by without him!

> **Top Tip:** *Not every mum or dad, at first sight of their baby, instantly falls in love with him. Like any relationship, this one has to be worked at.*

New mum Linda, remembers looking at her son in special care . . .

'He was in an incubator and I had gone down to feed him at about midnight. He was about 12 hours old by this time, and had been visited by grandparents, etc. The unit was quiet and one of the staff made me a coffee. As I sat on the chair in the gentle lamplight, looking at my tiny son struggling to breathe, I remember thinking "So you're mine. We've got to make a go of this, mate. I'll help you if you help me. We can do this together."

'I actually remember looking at his face with all his features and getting to know him. By the time I left the unit I really did love him, much more than when I had given birth to him. When they had first handed him to me, all I had thought was "I'm so tired, how could you have put me through all that?!".'

If you have a partner, remember that this baby is equally both of yours. Talk to each other about how you feel. A mum who appears totally enthralled by junior may secretly feel overwhelmed with the responsibility. A dad who appears disinterested, may really be feeling nervous and inadequate about handling a small baby.

This new relationship will also be easier to build once you're able to elicit some kind of response from your child, rather than just watching him sleep and feed all day. There are a few things you can try to see if you get a reaction:

- Look into your baby's face and deliberately stick your tongue out, waiting to see if he copies you (don't worry, though, if he doesn't immediately).
- Let him grasp hold of your finger placed into his hand.
- Stroke your baby's cheek. His head will turn as if he is looking to feed from the breast.

Your Baby's Health

All babies are examined by the midwife following delivery. This is a basic examination, checking there are no major abnormalities. It is usually relatively quick, so that baby can get back to being with mum and dad. A doctor – either the hospital paediatrician or your GP – will carry out a more detailed examination of the baby after at least six hours, but usually when baby is around 24 hours old.

Initially your baby may be covered in blood and vernix (the white lard-like stuff that covers their skin in the womb). If you have had a vaginal delivery, your baby's head may seem slightly out of shape; this is because the bones of the skull override each other due to the flexibility offered by the fontanelles (soft spots) at the front and back of their heads. This allows the diameter of your baby's skull to be as small as possible as it passes through the birth canal. Normal shape will be resumed shortly!

49

Mum's Postnatal Health

In addition to your tiredness following labour, if you have had an assisted delivery (breech, forceps or ventouse), or if you have had a perineal tear or an episiotomy (cut), you will have stitches and/or a bruise 'down below'. Deep bruises anywhere can hurt, but the location of this one can mean it will be particularly uncomfortable and make it difficult to sit down.

Even if you had a 'normal' delivery, with an intact perineum, it will take a while to feel everything is normal 'down there'! Initially, with or without stitches, passing urine can sting a bit because your wee is acidic and most women sustain grazes to their vaginal wall or perineum, even if they do not have any stitches. For many new mums, the discomfort can be greatly alleviated by drinking plenty of fluid to ensure their urine is as dilute as possible. If your discomfort is extreme, however, keep a large plastic jug in the toilet, fill it with warm water, sit back on the loo and pour the water between your legs as you pass urine. This washes the acidic urine away as rapidly as possible, reducing stinging. If the stinging persists for more than a day or two talk to your midwife. She may ask you to do a urine specimen to send to the laboratory, just to make sure you do not have a urinary tract infection.

Following the delivery you will also experience a blood loss, similar to a period. The length of time this lasts varies, but it will change colour over the course of a few days – from bright red, to pink, to brown. If it disappears, but then returns, or becomes red again, it is a sign that you are doing too much and should rest more.

Opening your bowels (doing a poo!) following delivery is an experience most women remember vividly! The midwives will ask you every day whether you have done this or not. If you do not go, or feel uncomfortable, they will offer you a mild laxative (which is safe for breastfeeding mothers to take). Many women find hospital food, and being less active, prevents them going to the toilet, as well as 'bashful bowel syndrome' – a preference for your own loo at home! A healthy diet of fresh fruit and vegetables, before and after the birth, should also help.

If you have delivered by Caesarean section, whether it is elective (planned) or an emergency (urgent or in labour), it's important to remember that you are recovering from major abdominal surgery, as well as having a new baby to deal with. The section may also have taken place at the end of an already long and tiring labour. You will be offered pain relief following this type of surgery and it's good to remember that there are no added Brownie points for bravery! If it hurts (and this goes for vaginal deliveries too), ask the midwives and doctors for something to help lessen the pain.

Much of the discomfort you feel post Caesarean will be caused by wind. This is because, frankly, your insides have been pulled about a fair bit! The best way to relieve this and get everything moving again, is to be active. Sarah, a new mum recalls:

'Our middle child was born by Caesarean, and I remember the tiniest healthcare assistant coming to me suggesting I have a shower. All I could think was, "I'll never manage it!"

'As she dashed away to make sure the bath did not overflow, I thought, "This is it! I must do this myself because, if I fall, I'll flatten her!" Before she got back in the room I was up on my feet – much to her amazement when she did return. It was the best thing I could have done. Although it's hard, at the time, to get moving soon after the operation, it really does make a difference if you can.'

No one is suggesting that you should get up, do a full aerobics class and then run round the block – you need to rest. Regular, short bouts of exercise, however, will undoubtedly help you recover more quickly.

You may also find that handling your baby after a Caesarean can be quite tricky! In hospital, the position and height of the cot, with the locker beneath, can cause a bit of a problem. Get someone to help you get out the things that you'll need regularly and put them where you can reach them easily. It's a good principle to apply when you get home, too. Keep all your nappy-changing things within easy reach, so you can get to them without stretching too much.

Learning the Ropes

For mums and dads, their contact with young babies, before becoming parents themselves, varies tremendously. A sense of nervousness at having to handle and care for a very small baby – even if it is your own – is perfectly natural. Inevitably, new mums tend to take the lead in looking after junior, but don't let that prevent *both* of you getting involved with baby care during the early days. For instance, workload permitting, midwives on postnatal wards usually encourage dads to bath the babies at weekends (this tends to be when the ward is full of men). Most dads' initial feelings of horror soon subside when they get into it; their confidence grows in leaps and bounds and, most importantly, everyone has great fun!

For the baby himself (assuming a fairly straightforward pregnancy and delivery), most of his first 24 hours will probably be spent asleep, interspersed with waking for feeding and the occasional nappy change. If this is the case for you, make the most of it and, while he naps, try to rest yourself.

Chapter 7 looks in more detail at the practicalities of day to day parenthood, but in the early days, your midwife, or the hospital staff, will help you get to grips with all of the basics. They will show you how to breastfeed or prepare feeds for the baby, bath him, 'top and tail' him, and all the other basic skills required to meet his needs.

There is a tendency for brand new parents to feel anxious that they should know all about every aspect of baby care from day one. The truth is, however, that you cannot possibly know everything, and certainly not until you've experienced being a parent for yourself!

 Top Tip: *However much previous experience they have had with children, both mums and dads have to learn new skills to care for a small baby. The best way to do it is to just get on with it!*

Don't be over concerned if things take a little while to get the hang of. For instance, babies and mums both need to get the 'knack' of feeding. It may not happen instantly, even though we often expect it to. The same is true for sleeping – particularly if there have been complications during the pregnancy or birth. For example, babies who have had a difficult forceps or ventouse delivery will sometimes object to being handled – they can be restless, sleep little and cry a lot. The main reason is that they have a *monumental* headache and, just like we would in the same situation, want to be left alone! In these circumstances, there is very little you can do except provide cuddles and reassurance where and when you can. Be guided by the midwives and nursery nurses looking after you both. They will have seen many babies struggle through the first hours after a difficult birth and are there to support and encourage you.

In the early days, the motto is '*Ask!*' Midwives, doctors and nursery nurses are there to help you gain confidence in handling your child, so ask them lots of questions, even if you feel stupid asking them! The important thing is that you are reassured about any worries you have and begin to feel confident about looking after your baby.

Top Tip: *Ask, ask, ask – it's what midwives and the other health professionals are there for.*

Length of Hospital Stay

The length of time you, and baby, stay in hospital will depend on how labour and delivery went. Obviously if you have had a Caesarean section, a ventouse (suction), forceps or breech delivery, you may need to stay in hospital longer than if you have had a 'normal' (spontaneous vaginal) delivery. Even so, there is tremendous variation in the time women spend in hospital with anything from six hours to six days being common.

There are many reasons why your return home may be delayed, including problems with baby. For example, some babies are reluctant to feed (this affects both breast- and bottle-fed babies) and, obviously, midwives would not want you to go home unless you were confident in handling and feeding your baby.

 Top Tip: *The length of hospital stay varies tremendously, so don't be disappointed if you end up staying longer than you had hoped.*

'Ooooh! Doesn't He Look Like You!'

How to Handle Visitors

Chances are, as soon as the baby arrives, lots of people will want to come and visit. Doting grandparents, brand new aunts and uncles, supportive friends and inquisitive neighbours all want a peek at the new arrival. It pays to have thought ahead about how you want to play things once the big day comes so that you can look after yourselves without the danger of offending anyone.

Of course, you will probably be keen, too, to show off your new arrival to all and sundry. And it's tremendously touching to know that people are interested enough in you and your baby to take the trouble to visit. The key, though, is *balance*. Entertaining visitors can be tiring at the best of times, especially if you're also trying to recover from labour and get to grips

with your new role as a mum or dad. It's important that you look after your baby's interests as well as your own – you're the parent now. Small babies can become fractious if constantly handed from person to person, especially if their sleep is disturbed. So, in the early days, your focus should be on avoiding the scenario where, at the end of visiting hours, you're exhausted from entertaining Uncle Tom Cobley and all, and still have to settle an unhappy baby.

 Top Tip: *It's always great to receive visitors, but make sure that they don't take control. You need to look after yourself and your baby, so you're the one in charge!*

57

Establishing Your Visitor Policy

If at all possible try to make sure that you've talked with your partner, and even potential visitors, about what you would like your 'visitor policy' (at least for the early days) to be. You can't get it all sewn up, of course – before the birth, you have no real idea about how you'll be feeling post labour – but it's far better to decide what you do and don't want before a tricky situation actually arises. It's also much fairer to everyone who wants to visit and less likely to offend Great Auntie Maud who just happens to turn up unannounced!

 Top Tip: If possible, talk with your partner before-hand about how you would like to deal with visitors in the early hours and days.

If you're in hospital, you're probably in a better position to control visitor numbers. Most maternity units have quite a strict visitor policy and the added bonus of midwives on hand who may occasionally suggest that mum needs to rest and that 'now might be a good time to leave'! A typical visitor policy restricts visitors to two at any one time, plus dad. The problem is, many women have a crowd waiting outside in the corridor, who all spend time nipping in and out! By the end of visiting a dozen or so people have all been in two at a time and mum is knackered!

As a general rule, children under 14 are not allowed to visit the maternity wards, unless the baby is their brother or sister. This is because small children are an infection risk – they've always got runny noses, etc.! Additionally, some units may restrict the handling of babies to the parents only (sometimes granny and grandad too).

Top Tip: *Find out your hospital's visitor policy and tell your family and friends.*

In the very early days when mum is still in hospital, set the ground rules. It's probably better to be fairly regimented about the number of visitors and the length of time they stay. The vast majority of visitors will understand and it is only by restricting the numbers of visitors that you will be able to get some time to yourselves and, consequently, a bit of flexibility to squeeze in the occasional extra visitor if you *really* feel up to it.

If, at any time, unwanted visitors arrive, or do not seem to want to leave, don't be afraid to ask the midwives to ask them to go.

 Top Tip: *Hospitals have visitor policies designed to help new mums and dads. If you don't feel able to ask someone to leave, ask a midwife to do it for you!*

Post-Caesarean Section

If you have had a Caesarean section, especially if it came at the end of a long labour, try to keep visitors to the absolute minimum for the first few days. You won't feel up to facing lots of people, especially if you have a catheter and intravenous infusion (drip). Your partner, any existing children, and possibly grandparents (if they just *can't* wait) should be just about all. If you decide to allow any other visitors, make sure they know it will be for 5–10 minutes only.

59

Grandparents

For many mums and dads of new parents, becoming 'Granny' or 'Grandad' is a fantastic, if daunting, privilege and so a bit of self-indulgence is perfectly reasonable. Grandparents can have a unique and very special relationship with their grandchildren and a new child is, quite rightly, a cause for celebration.

But despite this unique place within the newly extended family, grandparents don't have to be ever present, unless *you* want them to be. In fact, most new parents find that the new arrival results in one, or both, of two possible effects on the way that they relate to their own mum and dad:

1. First, there's the dawning realisation of what it means to become a mother or a father. As the latest addition to the 'new mum or dad club', you suddenly begin to appreciate what your mum and dad went through when they had you all those years ago! And you finally begin to see why your parents sometimes reacted in the way that they did to certain situations, and why they worried about you all the time!

2. Second, there's the feeling that you need to assert yourself as a new parent, without interference from others. *You're* the one who's responsible for raising this child and you've got to be able to do it on your own.

These two, almost conflicting, points of view can sometimes result in tricky situations, where mum or dad want to ask the grandparent's advice on issues, but never want to guarantee to follow their advice! Some mums and dads go as far as admitting that, in the first weeks and months, this paradoxical situation makes their own parents the 'trickiest' visitors! New parents complain that grandparents have forgotten just how tiring life is with a new baby – the women have forgotten all the bad bits about their own deliveries, and certainly how long it takes to fully recover from labour. There may be an element of truth in this, but it's worth remembering that many grandmothers had their babies in hospital when the average stay, following a *normal* delivery was 10 days! (Some midwives even recall couples leaving their babies in the hospital and having one last evening out on night nine before taking junior home!)

Even those who had their babies at home had far more support because mother, father, uncles and aunts and brothers and sisters all lived close by. Over the last thirty years or so, however, there has been a well-documented decline of community in the UK – families have never lived as far apart as they do today. Previous generations pulled hard on the 'extended family' in times of need, with everyone rallying round. Nowadays, with grandparents and other relatives perhaps hundreds of miles away, it is rare to see the 'extended' family function in this way.

If there is potential for a clash of cultures between you and your own parents (or in-laws), it may be a good idea to lay down – and carefully explain – some ground rules at the earliest opportunity. If possible, make sure that you have talked the issue over, beforehand, with your partner and that you are both unanimous on the best way to broach any potentially inflammatory issues. Once you are agreed on where you're coming from, bite the bullet! If your parents do something you do not approve of, tell them. There's really no getting away from it. And remember, if you don't do it at the beginning, it will only get harder to do later on! You may need to gently remind your parents that things have changed since you were little and, whilst the things they did for you obviously did you no harm, not all of them are acceptable today. Watch out for the practice of dipping dummies and fingers in sugar!

Top Tip: *It's only right that grandparents can become involved with their new grandchild if they want to be. But remember, you're the parent now!*

Step Families and Siblings

If you or your partner has other children from previous relationships it is really important to work out, right from the outset, the relationship these siblings will have with the new baby. When it comes to visiting, 'complicated' family situations inevitably require a higher level of coordination, especially if tensions exist between the various parties. If, however, your relationship is good with ex-partners, stepchildren and so on, the older children may want to be involved with the new baby. You will need to think through the consequences of this, and always reassure the existing children that they are loved and cherished. By involving your other children in the raising of your new baby – even if they don't live with you – you may be surprised to discover that it even brings you closer together.

'You've Called Him WHAT?'

Few things cause as much disagreement amongst family and friends as the subject of names. It is amazing how many couples are devastated by the response to the name for baby. A long silence, followed by 'Mmmmm . . . well it's unusual.'

It's all a matter of taste, really. You may think that 'Gorgonzola' is the most beautiful, perfect name for your new little cherub but, unfortunately, not everyone will necessarily agree!

Like flares, the fashion in names changes almost constantly. And not everyone's taste in fashion is the same – after all, you don't come across many Kylies or Jasons any more, but who knows when they might return?!

In addition to basic 'name fashion', there is occasionally an expectation that certain children may carry 'family' names into the next generation. This is probably most common for the first-born child within a family but, however it comes about, the dilemma is the same – family expectation versus your freedom to choose names that you really want. For some new mums and dads, it's simply not a problem. For others, however, 'inherited' names are to be resisted at all costs! Many parents compromise by resigning themselves, early on, to incorporating the name somehow (but often buried within a list of others: James Stephen David *Methusala*). This can be an effective way of keeping the peace. Other parents choose to resist the name altogether and fight it out when it comes to the crunch.

Whatever your feelings regarding names, probably the best

advice is simply to be prepared for a variety of views. To quote a well-known saying, 'You can't please all of the people all of the time', so choose names that you, as the parent, feel happy with. Unless you stick rigidly to very traditional names, you'll always be open to a variety of opinions, so stick to your guns! If there are sensitive family issues to deal with, deal with them sensitively. But if you really don't want your baby named after some distant elderly relative, make it clear right from the start. Don't let anyone presume the family tradition will continue, if you are absolutely sure it won't!

While others have had their chance to choose names in the past, now it is *your* turn. And be reassured, even the sceptics may learn, as they get to know your baby, to love the name you've chosen.

Whatever the issue, the real key to success with family and friends is to keep them involved. Ask for help and advice from people around you – as a new parent it's only wise to get input from people who've been where you are now and it helps others feel valued. But asking for advice shouldn't mean an open invitation to interfere. It is all a question of balance so be careful not to always involve one person, or group of people, to the neglect of others. And always allow time for yourselves, and space to make your own decisions.

 Top Tip: *Whatever the issue, ask advice, but never be afraid to make, and stand by, your own decisions. After all, your child's upbringing is ultimately* your *responsibility.*

Once at Home

Once you return from the hospital, or if you've had your baby at home, it is even more important to regulate the number of visitors, as they can turn up at any time – and stay for ages! Unfortunately, it always seems to be those you most want to see who stay away, or who restrict themselves regarding visiting. Do not be afraid to defer visitors, both in hospital and at home. You may find you want to see a few people every day, or you might prefer visitors on alternate days.

Try to avoid booking up all of dad's holiday or paternity leave with visitors every day. You need time together, to adjust to your new roles and get to know your baby.

If friends want to visit, encourage them to call first and check

WE'D LOVE YOU TO COME ROUND AND HELP WITH THE BABY. COULD YOU ALSO WALK OUR DOG? –

FANG

it is OK. Avoid planning too far ahead – you won't know for sure how you're going to feel from day to day. And if you need something from the shops, and a friend calls to ask if they can visit, why not get them to pick up whatever you need on their way over?

One new mum found her 'best' visitor was a work colleague, who called by for half an hour after work. She brought a bag full of clothes her youngest child had grown out of but, best of all, she brought a huge casserole of bolognese. 'Just add spaghetti', she said! Marvellous!

 Top Tip: *The best visitors are the ones who aren't afraid to help out and who are happy to offer advice but don't expect you to always take it!*

Rules of Thumb

Just a few more 'visitor' top tips:

- There is nothing like a new baby to bring forward loads of advice from everyone. Listen to it all, smile sweetly, thank the person profusely, and then work out what works for you and your new family. On the whole, less advice is offered with subsequent children!
- Encourage people who have been unwell, especially with anything infectious, not to visit until they are fully recovered. If they do call round, dissuade them from handling baby, especially if they have an upset stomach or heavy cold, or any other more serious condition.
- Always remember that real friends won't mind being asked *not* to come round because you are tired, or your baby is

unsettled. Most people will want to catch you at your best anyway – as a happy, confident mother or father – not someone barely able to keep their eyes open, or string a few words together!

Top Tip: *Resist the temptation to book up all dad's paternity leave or holiday with visits from family and friends. This is a very special time, so make time for just your new family to be alone together.*

'Welcome to the Family . . .'

Arriving Home as a New Parent

Even if you have memorised, word for word, 'The A–Z Bumper Book of Parenting', nothing will completely prepare you for the moment when you shut your front door and you are left on your own for the first time. Whether you're a single parent, or living with your partner, you may well ask yourself, 'Help! What do I do now?'

Talk to anyone who has experienced it and they will instantly recall how vividly they remember either taking their first child home, or the moment when the midwife left following a home birth. Suddenly all the anticipation and excitement is over – it's just you and junior. Many new parents find themselves sitting on the sofa, looking at this amazing little person (normally sleeping peacefully as the result of a car journey home), and wondering how on earth they will cope without an instruction manual! Even experienced midwives, well used to the demands of small babies by the time they themselves became parents,

Welcome to the Family...'

WE'RE HOME AT LAST!
THIS IS WHERE OUR 'FIRST
SIX WEEKS' REALLY BEGINS.

...AND HOW MANY OF THEM DO YOU TWO PLAN TO WASTE STARING AT ME?

recollect their feelings of nervousness and thinking, 'Goodness, this one's mine! It's permanent!'

For many parents, being back in the familiar surroundings of home provides the first real chance to reflect on what has happened. While the baby sleeps, you can reflect all day! The problems start when, first, there is a whimper, then there's a little cry, then he really lets rip and his cry rises to an eardrum-piercing crescendo. All of sudden, it is up to you to take control and *do* something.

The BBC is always rerunning the vintage TV comedy, *Dad's Army*, which tells the story of a platoon of the Home Guard during World War II. One of the best-known characters is Corporal Jones, a veteran of many conflicts who, at the merest hint of danger, rushes about yelling 'DON'T PANIC! DON'T PANIC!' Of course, the irony is that Corporal Jones himself is the only one who ever actually seems to panic anyway! As a new parent, avoid 'Corporal Jones Syndrome' and, however hard it seems, try to relax. Panic only blinds you to the obvious, so breathe deeply and try to make a considered response to the situation. Remember crying is your baby's only means of getting

69

your attention. Babies are quite tuned in to your emotions, so the more relaxed you can be, the more contented a baby you'll have. As we saw at the very beginning of the book, billions of parents have got to grips with the early days of parenthood and – although you may not feel it at the moment – you can too!

 Top Tip: When you first come home from hospital, and the front door clicks shut, don't panic! Concentrate instead on making things easier for yourself.

Make life as easy as you can for you and your baby. Chapters 7, 8 and 9 look at the practicalities of baby care and the health of your new family, but in the meantime, here are some handy hints.

Handy Hints for the First Day or So at Home

1. **Give yourselves a bit of time**
    It is very important that once you arrive home you have time to get to know your baby and establish yourselves in your new role as a parent. When you first get home, make yourself a cup of tea, take the phone off the hook (or put the answerphone on), sit down and give yourself a minute or two to take stock.

2. **Rest where and when you can**
    As much as possible, forget the housework and other chores for a while. Wear clothes that you feel good in, but which are easy to clean and do not need much ironing. It

may sound silly, but see if you can arrange to have your hair cut – you'll be amazed at how much better a bit of pampering (however small) will make you feel!

Top Tip: *Give the housework a miss for a while. Use any free time to pay a bit of attention to yourself.*

---

3. **'Sleep, feed, change; sleep, feed, change . . .'**
    Be prepared for this cycle to become your primary focus and main activity for a little while! With this in mind:

    • If your home is on more than one floor, consider having two 'changing stations' – one upstairs, one down. You don't need a complete set of everything in both places, but being able to do the basics on either floor will considerably reduce the number of times you go up and down the stairs. This is particularly important for mums during the first few weeks – regardless of the type of delivery you've had, you will need time to recover.
    • Particularly if you are breastfeeding, decide where in your home – and in what position – you feel most comfortable feeding your baby. This could be a chair, the sofa, or even your bed. Until you are confident about feeding him anywhere, you may find it best to head for this place whenever your baby needs a feed.
    • Sleep, as much as possible, when your baby sleeps. However good he is, in the early days your baby is unlikely to sleep all night, so it's important you catch up when you can.

4. **Keep control over the flow of visitors**
   Some people feel inundated with visitors from the moment they return home, with many resorting to taking the phone off the hook and removing the batteries from the doorbell! This may be a good time to invest in an answering machine, if you do not already have one. At least this means you can screen the calls!

   As long as you assure those closest to you that you will contact them should you need too, you won't offend anyone. Those with your best interests at heart won't mind if you make them wait a day or two before they can visit (also see Chapter 4).

   One community midwife went round to see a new mum and was greeted by a huge sign on the front door that read:

Thank you for calling.
Mother, Father and baby son sleeping,
PLEASE DO NOT DISTURB.
Leave your name below, and we will get back to you.
Thank you so much for your kind consideration.

The poor midwife was not too sure what to do! Eventually she knocked on the door, and the (somewhat embarrassed) dad was at great pains to say he hadn't meant to exclude the very person they were waiting for!

 Top Tip: *Don't be afraid to be honest with those around you. If you don't want visitors, say so – put them off until another day.*

---

5. **Enlist help**

At the same time as controlling social visitors, now is the time to call upon all those people you (or someone else) enlisted as helpers to swing into action. A daily hot meal delivered (as long as it's not shepherd's pie *every* day) is great. The occasional sack of laundry, washed and ironed, is brilliant. The shopping done is a godsend. Make the most of it – you don't have a baby every day and the willing volunteers won't be round for long! If you haven't had the chance to get any help sorted out beforehand, there may be a good friend you can ask to coordinate things on your behalf. You'll be amazed how people respond – they love rallying round and they like to be asked!

6. **Use the professionals**

Remember there are lots of professionals on hand to help every parent during the first years of parenthood:

- *Midwives* have a professional responsibility for new mums and babies up until 28 days after the birth. Whether you deliver at home or in hospital, you are usually given a list of phone numbers to call any time of the day or night, if you are concerned about yourself or baby. Midwives call on you once you are at home, certainly during the first 10 days of your baby's life. The frequency of these visits will depend on you and your baby. Although they will visit right up until the 28th day if necessary, after 10 days (or so, depending on when weekends and public holidays fall) they hand over your care to the health visitor.
- *Health visitors* are nurses who have undertaken some obstetric training, and may well have completed midwifery training, in addition to specialist health visiting training. It is the health visitor who has professional responsibility for your baby until he is five years old. They will advise you

about things like feeding, weaning (when the time comes) and baby clinics, and will regularly weigh your baby. They give advice on and undertake immunisation programmes and will also perform developmental and hearing checks to ensure your baby is developing normally. They work Monday to Friday, 9 (ish) to 5 (ish).

CAT FLAP? NO THAT'S THE 'MIDWIFE GP AND HEALTH VISITORS' FLAP.

- **Your GP** *(family doctor)* is often your first port of call if you are at all worried about your baby's health. Many GPs will visit a new mum and her baby within a few days of either delivery or transfer home. In many areas, it is the GP who does the six-week postnatal check for the mum as well as the six-week baby check. Many mums spend quite a lot of time in the GP surgery – either to see a doctor or a practice nurse. One woman, with two small children, commented while visiting the doctor one day that she did not know why they were paying a mortgage on a house, as she spent most of her time in the GP surgery with one son or the other!

- *Mother And Baby Emergency Line (MABEL)* or similar. Many hospitals will give you a contact number to call if you are at all concerned about baby or mum. Often you will only need a bit of reassurance, but these services provide a midwife always available at the end of a phone. She can organise another midwife to call on you, advise you to contact your GP, or ask you to come into the hospital.
- *NHS Direct.* Many areas offer a telephone advice service through NHS direct. If you are uncertain as to whether to contact your GP or hospital, a quick call to NHS direct can be very helpful.
- *Your pharmacist.* If you are unsure about whether to consult your GP, or want advice regarding medicines suitable for baby, ask your local pharmacist. They are a great source of knowledge, but if they can't help you, they will simply refer you back to your GP or health visitor.

 Top Tip: Make good use of the professional advice and support available to you. Doctors, midwives, health visitors and others are all there to help.

---

7. **Go easy on yourself**
   It's common for new parents to feel totally at sea and overwhelmed with the responsibility of a new baby. This is often even more apparent in men and women who are a little older when they have their babies, or have carved out a career for themselves before children come on the scene. This could be because they have become used to being in

control and being competent at what they do. They are acclimatised to deciding what needs doing, who should be doing it, how it should be done, and when by. But suddenly the whole world has shifted. This little burping, squealing bundle is calling the shots now, and all of a sudden they're not in control any longer and don't quite know what to do! Whether this applies to you or not, go easy on yourself and try to enjoy it (you'll be amazed, but it is possible!).

Top Tip: *Even if you feel overwhelmed at first, try to relax. You can do it!*

A Special Word about Our Furry Friends

If you have a pet that has been your pride and joy until junior comes along, be careful how you play things when you arrive home. Whilst your pet buffalo won't be bothered much, and your goldfish couldn't be any *less* interested, the same cannot necessarily be said for your average pet dog or cat. Although, undoubtedly, pets can be a bonus in any family with growing children, new mums and dads with pets should take several, very basic precautions.

Dogs
- On arrival home from hospital with the baby, make sure you walk in first, but *not* holding him. Make a fuss of the dog, and let someone else bring in the baby behind you.
- As soon as the baby needs changing, make sure you do it on a changing mat (or towel) on the floor, so the dog can

see exactly what is going on. Let someone else hold the dog's collar so he can't lick or sniff the baby all over!

- It may sound disgusting, but give your dog the dirty nappy and let him sniff it (you might want to do this outside, dependent on how dirty the nappy is!) The dog will want to find out what the baby is, and can best do this by using his sense of smell. Once he's familiar with your baby's smell, and realises that this is a new, important member of your family, he will be less likely to view the baby as a threat.

- However good your dog appears to be with your baby *never* leave them alone together. It is simply too much responsibility for the dog!

- Avoid letting your dog lick your child, especially around his face and hands.

- Never let your dog lick any of the baby's equipment. One midwife recalls being horrified as a junior student midwife, when visiting one new mum in London. She watched as the young mum made up a bottle feed (in a not terribly clean kitchen) and then held the bottle for the German shepherd dog to lick, before plunging it into the mouth of her three-day-old baby. As the midwife stood completely speechless, her older, more experienced, colleague casually suggested that this was probably not a good idea and perhaps it would be better not to give the baby's bottle to the dog. It turned out that this was the only way that the mum had thought of to stop the dog being jealous!

Cats

The same general principles apply, but it is also worth mentioning that:

- Cat nets are available from most baby care shops. Cats often like to climb into cots and prams with babies. This is

77

because small babies are warm and smell of milk. There have always been fears that, when this happens, a cat will smother a baby but, in fact, it is more a problem of hygiene.

- During pregnancy, most women avoid contact with cats and cat litter, due to the possibility of toxoplasmosis – a condition that is spread by cat poo – which causes health problems for the developing baby. Likewise new babies are susceptible to the illnesses spread by other animals.

General Precautions

- If you have young children, it is advisable to keep your pet vaccinations up to date, not only to protect your pet, but also your children.
- If you have an unusual pet you should speak to your veterinary surgeon about any specific precautions you may need to take. We know of at least one parrot that sulked for weeks when a new baby came home!

Top Tip: *Introduce your pet to your new baby gently and never leave them alone with your child – it puts too much responsibility on the animal.*

A Life Less Ordinary

Special Care Babies and Multiple Births

In addition to the pressures and anxieties experienced by all parents to one degree or another, some new mums and dads face more challenges than most as they enter parenthood. The material contained elsewhere in this book should be relevant in all circumstances, but this chapter takes a brief, additional look at some of the issues faced by parents if they:

- have a baby who arrives prematurely, or requires admission to a Neonatal Intensive Care or Special Care Baby Unit,
- have twins, triplets, or more.

Premature and Special Care Babies

Most babies are born between the 39th and 41st weeks of pregnancy. If, however, a baby is born before the 37th completed week it is said to be 'pre-term or premature'. *Very* early babies (those born as much as ten, or more, weeks early) often need lots of medical intervention to help them survive the first few weeks of life. They are likely to go into a Special Care Baby Unit (SCBU – often known colloquially, because of the initials, as a 'scaboo'), or even the Neonatal Intensive Care Unit (NICU). Additionally, for numerous reasons, any baby (born at any gestation) can be placed in special care. Babies born after about 34 weeks, though fulfilling the definition of 'premature', do not *always* go to SCBU/NICU.

Babies are born early for a whole host of reasons, but these include:

- Mum simply going into labour and delivering with very little, or even no, warning.
- Mum having a medical condition that necessitates early delivery to ensure she and the baby are in good health (e.g. diabetes mellitus).
- Specific conditions within pregnancy that require delivery to avoid possible negative implications for the wellbeing of either the baby or the mother. Such conditions include pre-eclampsia (characterised by high blood pressure and protein in the mother's urine); eclampsia (fits), HELLP Syndrome (a complication of pre-eclampsia or eclampsia that causes liver problems); and obstetric cholestasis (itching in pregnancy).
- Having twins, triplets etc.

Nursing and medical staff in SCBU/NICU are used to all these different scenarios and will help you both to cope in this situation.

Adjusting to the fact you are a parent weeks before you were expecting to be can be hard. A premature baby makes premature parents. The key to coping in such a difficult situation

is trying to enlist help. As much as you can, get someone else to look after the other important aspects of your life (friends, family etc.), leaving you to concentrate on the health and wellbeing of yourself and your baby.

> **Top Tip:** If your baby goes into special care, try to get someone to help you look after the other important aspects of your life outside the hospital.

No one enjoys having their newborn baby ensconced on SCBU. During antenatal tours around maternity units many couples choose not to see Special Care – the logic being, if they don't go there, nor will their baby! Unfortunately, for obvious reasons, this is not always the case, sometimes meaning that subsequent admission to the unit is more traumatic than necessary. Mums and dads with a special care baby may not be able to get close to him, or cuddle him very much, if at all. And seeing your tiny child completely overwhelmed with machines can be distressing for anybody, let alone a new parent. He seems so small and everything around him seems so big.

It can help to know exactly what each machine, or tube, does, so make sure that you ask the staff to talk you through every bit of equipment. Ask, ask, ask.

 Top Tip: Don't be intimidated by all the equipment in a SCBU. If you want to know what something does, ask!

Special Care Dads
It can be a particularly difficult time for a new dad, adjusting to his new role as a parent, with a baby in SCBU and a partner who is also unwell. In many situations, mum will stay in hospital with the baby, which will mean, in turn, dad spends a lot of time on his own, racing around, to and from the hospital. It's easy for him to feel exhausted, lonely and desperately anxious. Dads can feel guilty about not being able to be at the hospital all the time and, even when they are there, they are unsure whether they should be with their partner or with their baby.

> **Top Tip:** *It's easy for dads with special care babies to feel torn in every direction. You can't be everywhere, though, so do what you can and don't feel guilty about things you are powerless to do anything about.*

If you're a dad with a partner in hospital and a baby in SCBU:

- Accept help from those around you, especially close family and friends.
- Spend more of your time with your partner. Your baby will be receiving all the care he needs and, in any case, very premature babies often do not like excessive handling, even if they are well enough to be held.
- Encourage friends and family to cook at least one meal a day for you! This means you not only have a proper meal, but also maintain a modicum of normality.
- However difficult it seems, make sure you get enough sleep.
- If you work, talk to your employer – routine paternity leave may be relaxed in this situation. That said, however, many fathers discover it's better to keep working while baby is in hospital, and take annual or paternity leave once he is discharged home.
- If your absence from work causes financial problems, talk to your bank or mortgage provider sooner rather than later.

Hospitals with NICU/SCBUs

The treatment babies need varies tremendously, as does the length of time they need to stay in the unit. Additionally, due to the way that neonatal care is organised, not every hospital has intensive care cots, and those that do only have a limited number. Consequently if a problem is suspected it can mean a mum is transferred to another hospital prior to having her baby, or that her baby is transferred soon after delivery. Whenever possible, this transfer is to the nearest hospital able to provide the specialised care that you and your baby need. But sometimes, local resources simply cannot provide what is necessary, and you can end up a long way from home. This can make visiting difficult but, all being well, as soon as your baby is strong enough he will be transferred back to your local hospital.

As much as possible, the staff in SCBU/NICU will involve you in your baby's care. Some of the nurses working there will be midwives and others will be general nurses and nursery nurses. They have all chosen to work in this area and will have received lots of specialist training in how best to care for tiny babies. They will help mums use breast pumps to express breast milk if their baby is too small or unwell to feed from the breast.

Ten Special Top Tips for Special Care Parents

1. Be prepared for how small a premature baby can be. Many new parents think an 8 lb (3.5 kg) baby is tiny, so if your baby is 4 lb (under 2 kg) he really will be very little indeed and, as a result, other people around you may be very reluctant to handle him. Remind yourself that even relatively 'large' premature babies look tiny when surrounded by all the equipment used in SCBU.

2. Although you, as a mum or dad, will be positively encouraged to come and go as you please, remember that other visitors may be restricted. Check with the staff as to who is allowed to visit and when – this will prevent unnecessary visits, and potentially awkward situations. With the proviso that they themselves are not ill with colds,

fevers, etc., most units will allow visits (at pre-allotted times) from grandparents and the baby's brothers or sisters.

3. Take lots of photos every day. Babies change daily, and everyone will want to see pictures, especially if they are not able to visit.

4. Keep in close contact with one particular relative or friend near home. They will then be able to deal with calls from everyone else.

5. For both you and your partner, use the time that your baby remains in hospital to recover from the delivery. Avoid the temptation to rush around doing everything, and then visiting baby as well.

6. Ask, ask, ask. Talk to the neonatal nurses, midwives and doctors, so you feel you really know how your baby is doing.

7. Many units will ask mum to move into a small room close to the main SCBU for a couple of days before baby is fit for discharge. This will enable you to care for your baby with the support of the staff.

8. Prepare yourself for the possibility that, as a new mother, you may be discharged from hospital before your baby. This can be especially emotionally tough – probably the last thing you expected would be to go home without him. If you do come home without your baby, try to line up plenty of people to give you lifts to and from the hospital – you probably won't feel up to much driving.

9. As a new parent, take into account the other suggestions (regarding visitors, diet, exercise and life in general) contained in this book. Nearly all of it still applies!

10. If your baby was born early due to you having a medical condition, or because your baby was not growing well, you may want to discuss the chances of having problems

in a subsequent pregnancy with your obstetrician, or other relevant clinical specialist. There are also numerous organisations who support families who have been through these types of problems, and who also fund research into specific conditions (see the useful addresses section at the back of this book).

Alex's story

Jacqui and her partner, Peter, had gone to the New Forest for their last holiday before the baby arrived. Jacqui awoke at 3 a.m. when her 'waters' broke. She was 32 weeks and 5 days into her pregnancy. They had to decide what to do. They had no idea where the nearest hospital was so decided to head back home to Kent. The landlady at the B&B was disturbed by their frantic attempts to get out of the hotel! She thought they were burglars!

They dashed back to Kent through the night, arriving just 45 minutes before their son was born. Jacqui had the briefest of cuddles, and Alex was whisked off to Special Care. Initially he did well, but gradually tired and needed extra help with his breathing, which resulted in his being put on a ventilator. Both parents found this very traumatic, seeing their tiny son surrounded with the tubes needed to keep him alive.

Looking back now, Jacqui can clearly recall life on the postnatal ward. Sharing a six-bedded bay with other mothers, she often felt very lonely; all the other mums had non-special care babies, who slept in cots at the foot of their mums' beds and kept them awake at night, whereas her baby was in another part of the hospital.

She often felt frightened by all the equipment keeping her son alive. At one point, at Jacqui's request, the hospital chaplain came and blessed Alex. Jacqui had thought this would be comforting, but in reality she felt as though she had allowed him to have the last rite!

Jacqui did not get to cuddle her son until he was three days old. The staff had realised how desperate she was to hold him and so one of the nurses ventilated him by hand while Jacqui held him, as he still wasn't able to breathe on his own. Fortunately for Jacqui and Peter, a little girl in the same unit was a day older than Alex. Alex's progress appeared to mimic hers and so they felt they were forewarned about what was to follow from one day to the next.

Jacqui went home after five days, leaving Alex in hospital. She spent most of her time travelling back and forth, but longed to show her baby off to friends and family. Visitors were strictly limited on SCBU, so Jacqui felt deprived of all the 'oohs' and 'aahs' from well-wishers! After three weeks, however, Alex had got his act together and Jacqui and Peter were able to take him home.

Today Alex is a large, happy, healthy three-year-old, who has just had a new baby sister, Emma, born at – yes, you guessed it – 32 weeks and 5 days! She also spent her first two weeks in Special Care. Despite their son being whisked away at delivery, Jacqui and Peter have not experienced any problems in 'bonding' with either their son or daughter. And having been through it once before, they were certainly both more confident with Emma, and better able to cope with the trials and tribulations of an early baby in SCBU.

 Top Tip: *Seeing your baby in SCBU can be worrying for any parent. Once they come out, though, there's no reason for you to experience any long-term problems in bonding with your child.*

Multiple Births

Not every parent arrives home with only one baby! Twins are born in about one in 80 pregnancies and triplets occur once in about every 300 pregnancies. And, partly due to the success of infertility treatment, the numbers are growing! Again, most of the advice within this book applies to any number of children, but it goes without saying that multiple births bring their own, very specific challenges! If you have had twins or triplets you will need lots and lots of help to look after two, three – even four or five – babies, who will often demand attention at, or around, the same time!

 Top Tip: More than one baby really does mean you need lots of help in the first few weeks.

Handy Hints for Mums and Dads with More than One Baby
Below are some Top Tips from seasoned 'multiple' parents:

FEEDING
- Some mums very successfully breastfeed more than one baby. A triangular pillow is a good investment for any mum, but even more valuable if you are feeding more than one, because you can put it on your lap so that it supports the babies. This makes it much easier to feed them both at the same time. Triangular pillows are widely available, but vary greatly in price – so, if possible, shop around!
- If you are bottle-feeding twins (or triplets), buy two (or three) different coloured bottle tops, and always use a different colour for each baby. This means that when you are feeding the babies simultaneously, and stop to wind one, you will not get confused as to which bottle belongs to whom! Later on, when you reach the weaning stage, you may find it easier to make up one large bowl of food, and feed all the children from the same spoon. It avoids confusion for you and their resistance to infection will be much improved by then. In any case, if one gets a cold they probably all will anyway!

BATHING
- Invest in a couple of 'baby sponges' – the large sponges with a baby shape cut out. Mums and dads say they work because they allow them to bath both babies simultaneously in a normal bath. One baby is supported on the sponge whilst the other is being washed.

EQUIPMENT AND CLOTHING

- It may sound obvious, but you do not need twice as much equipment for twins (or three times as much for triplets, etc.). But even though you probably won't need it all, many parents of twins are totally amazed at the amount of stuff they are given. It seems that everyone loves a new baby, but a multiple birth is a licence to really splash out!

- If you have same-sex twins or triplets, and do not want them to be dressed identically, do tell those around you. If you don't, you risk being given the same outfit for each child. The same thing goes for toys. Often well-meaning family and friends will give each child identical gifts. Sometimes that is fine, but there are some things you really only need one of! Two (or more) 'super-massive, ride-on, off-road diggers' can seem *huge* in even the largest of living rooms!

GETTING OUT

- New mums and dads with twins (or triplets) often leave it quite a while after the birth before going out alone with their babies, and tend to get anxious about that first trip. The consensus of opinion, however, from parents who have been in this situation, seems to be that it is better to get on with it, and that it never proves to be as difficult as you imagined (although most new parents of twins do not appear to venture much onto public transport!). Be prepared, though, for very slow outings in the early days. It takes a long time to get out of the house and, once you're out, everyone wants to stop you and admire your babies!

PRAMS AND BUGGIES

- Prams and buggies are a major consideration (and investment) for every new parent, but especially when you're finding the best 'wheels' for more than one baby! Many parents in this position end up with an array of prams which, in total, add up to a hefty outlay. One couple discussed the problems of twins and prams, after confessing to having four! They have:

1. first, a tandem buggy – one in front of the other (but as the girls have got older they've learnt to kick each other),
2. second, a side by side buggy (which they think is the best), and
3. finally, two single buggies, for when they are out as a family, with friends who can push one, or going somewhere not wide enough for the side by side buggy. They occasionally also use one of these when either parent is out, putting one baby in a sling and the other in a buggy.

It is a wonder they can get through their front door at all! There are no absolute, sure-fire winners for solving these problems – it's just a case of finding what works best for you and making sure that it's within your budget. General 'buggy principles' (like shopping around, making sure it fits your lifestyle and isn't too big to fit, for example, into your car) are contained in the chapter on Great Expectations (Chapter 2). Strangely enough, however, one extra tip worth noting is that there is usually a lot more choice in mainland Europe. UK stores often stock only a very limited selection of twin and triplet buggies, so if you're feeling adventurous (and need an excuse), why not consider a day trip to France? Even if you don't actually buy the one you want while you're there (although they're often cheaper than at home), you will at least see a wider variety from which you can then order your choice once back in the UK. Of course if you *do* buy a buggy when you're over there, you can also use it to wheel back the wine, beer and cheese that you'll have acquired!

Top Tip: *When it comes to parenting twins and triplets, ask other parents who have experienced it about what worked and what didn't. Ask at the antenatal, or child health, clinic about a local Twins and Multiple Birth self-help group.*

Shopping

Upon hearing that, as a parent of twins less than six weeks old, you're thinking about going shopping, some people's immediate reaction might be to shout, 'ARE YOU MAD? GET SOMEONE ELSE TO DO IT FOR YOU!' They may have a point – negotiating the weekly shop may not be the most stress-free exercise. On the other hand, however, as time passes you probably won't always have someone nearby to help you out when you need it. Similarly, you may feel that hitting the shops is part of getting back to normality and be keen to face the challenge. So if you simply *have* to go shopping:

- Check out your local supermarkets to see which are 'twin friendly' (a very common complaint amongst parents of twins). See how many of your store's trolleys are suitable for more than one small baby. Many parents have headed to their regular supermarket, only to find there is just one trolley they could use to safely seat both babies, and someone else is using it! If mum or dad are by themselves they may have no alternative but to go elsewhere. If this happens to you, go to the 'Customer Services' counter and explain your predicament – after all the shop can't sort out the problem if they don't know it exists! There does not appear to be a particular supermarket that is consistently better than the others at looking after parents with more than one baby – it seems to be all about location!

- If you have a computer at home, consider doing your food shopping via the Internet. This will save you time, and the delivery charge may only be a fraction of the cost of the bus fare or petrol you use travelling from supermarket to supermarket trying to find the right sort of trolley for your twins. The added bonus, of course, is that they deliver right to your door and, in many cases, right into your kitchen. With any luck, one day, they may even put it away for you!

 Top Tip: If you simply have to go shopping, set yourself realistic goals for what you want to achieve.

Early Days

Down to Practicalities

The baby's arrived, the cards and flowers are out on display, you've got your visitors sussed, a hot meal is being delivered daily! Now you've got yourself sorted out, though, it's time to think about this little baby and the practicalities of caring for him.

This chapter looks at:

1. Feeding – breast and bottle
2. Changing nappies
3. Sleep
4. Cord care
5. Bath time
6. Crying
7. Going out

 Top Tip: When your baby is small, the list of things for you to learn can seem enormous. But rest assured, within a few weeks you'll wonder what all the fuss was about!

As adults we accept we all have different temperaments, but research by Judith Lauwers and Candace Woessner in the 1990s defined various baby 'types' in order to help parents cope with the very individual needs of their child:

- *Average baby.* This baby sleeps 12–20 hours a day and feeds 6–14 times. When awake, he is usually quiet, listens to the noises around him and responds to them. He also enjoys being handled. If he is unhappy he will try and console himself by, for example, sucking his fist.
- *Easy baby.* This child sleeps for longer stretches and feeds 6–14 times a day. He is generally very easy to please.
- *Placid baby.* These babies sleep 18–20 hours a day and may only feed 4–6 times a day. When they are awake these children are calm and placid, making few demands for attention.

- *Active/fussy baby (sometimes also known as 'high need' babies).* They need far less sleep than children in any of the other groups. They feed more frequently, tending to eat and sleep in irregular patterns. When awake they demand attention, but seem to dislike new situations. They cry quite frequently and are unable to console themselves.

1. Feeding

Regardless of whether you decide to breast- or bottle-feed your baby, feeding will take up a lot of your time in these early weeks – it'll seem like it's all you do! Particularly as a breast-feeding mum, it can be easy to feel like you've turned into nothing more than a glorified milk machine, or as one dad put it, a 'meals on slippers' service! Even for bottle-fed babies, the constant round of washing and sterilising bottles and making up feeds can occupy you for hours on end!

Baby Weight

Babies are usually weighed around 10 days after birth, and it's not unusual for them to be fractionally below their birth weight. Most babies lose weight in the first few days of life (up to 10 per cent of their birth weight is common), but this is usually regained by around day 10. As long as your baby was born at term (or thereabouts), is healthy, feeding regularly, and settling in between feeds, he'll be doing fine. If your baby was born early (before 37 weeks), was small (under 2.5 kg), is jaundiced or has any other problem, the midwives and doctors will advise you further regarding feeds.

Many books suggest that babies grow at a constant rate. However experience (and some more enlightened books) point to the fact that, in truth, babies grow at erratic rates. Some weeks you will take your baby along to the baby clinic to be weighed, thinking you have done nothing but feed him, and the health visitor or practice nurse will tell you he hasn't put on much weight. Try not to feel disheartened. At other times, he will have experienced a growth spurt and you'll be deliriously happy!

 Top Tip: *Babies put on weight fairly erratically. Sometimes he will have gained a lot, while at other times, very little. Neither need be a cause for concern.*

Breast or Bottle

Many women know, deep down, whether they want to breast- or bottle-feed their baby. For others, it poses a dilemma. During the last 10–15 years there has been a high profile campaign to encourage women to breastfeed. This campaign has gained momentum as research has shown that 'breast is best', providing babies with perfect food for their nourishment and development.

A less fortunate by-product, however, from the successful communication of the 'breast is best' message is that women who cannot, or choose not to, breastfeed can feel like 'second class' mothers. Consequently, they sometimes feel awkward about telling midwives that they do not intend to breastfeed. Some have even been known to breastfeed in hospital, only to switch to bottle-feeding once home. Don't be embarrassed about your decision – the last thing you need, immediately after labour, is to be anxious about what other people think. And anyway, your midwife will want to support you regardless of the option you take.

If you are unsure about feeding, talk to your midwife before or after the birth. If you think breastfeeding might suit you, though, give it a try! Many women, adamant before the birth about their preferred method of feeding, change their mind once their baby is born. At the end of the day, however, there may be many reasons why you decide that breastfeeding really isn't for you. It may be physical, cultural, social, or just personal. Whatever the reasons, don't waste time and energy feeling bad about opting for the bottle – babies are small for only a very short time and you don't want those days to be filled with guilt for you. If you can breastfeed – great! If not, relax – none of us has the way we were fed as babies tattooed on our foreheads!

Remember, too, that midwives and other nursing staff in hospitals are there to help you feed your baby – whichever way you choose to do it. Their aim is to help new parents grow in confidence in the early days. So be honest, and, whether breastfeeding or bottle-feeding, use their professional experience and advice to learn, for yourself, the skills to do it properly.

 Top Tip: *Choose the method of feeding that suits you best. If you decide to breastfeed – great! If you would prefer to bottle-feed – fine! Don't be embarrassed about your decision.*

Breastfeeding

If you can do it, breastfeeding is *brilliant* – a natural, convenient (and cheap) way to give your baby everything he needs early on. However, initially, breastfeeding is also incredibly hard work as you and your baby slowly get the hang of it. Expectant mums and dads aren't ever prepared for this – many assume it's an instinct, which should come, well, *naturally*. To a certain extent, of course, it does, but don't be surprised if mum and junior take a week or 10 days to really get into the swing of it! You are both learning a new skill and, as with anything new, it does take time.

 Top Tip: *The first 7–10 days of breastfeeding are always the hardest. But hang in there and, by two weeks, you'll be amazed at how much easier it seems!*

Whether at home or in hospital, midwives and nurses are there to offer you support, encouragement and practical advice as you begin to breastfeed. So make the most of them by asking lots of questions – repeatedly, if you are unsure. For instance, correctly positioning your baby (and you) will prevent you suffering sore nipples and other aches and pains – again, your midwife will show you how. Ensuring baby 'fixes' well (meaning he has your nipple and the surrounding area correctly in his mouth), will mean he will get a good feed which, in turn, will stimulate your breast to produce more milk.

For the first few days, the breast only produces colostrum (first milk). This is very nutritious, passing on immunity to many common illnesses (colds, etc.) as well as the easily digestible food he needs to thrive. This only lasts two or three days, so even if you manage only to breastfeed for a few days, it can still have a long-term impact upon your child's health. Some cultures, on the other hand, frown upon feeding their babies colostrum, as they believe this first milk is 'dirty'. Instead, they commence breastfeeding once their milk has come in. There is no evidence that these babies are more at risk from infection, etc. because they do not get this nutritious food, although these cultures often breastfeed their children for quite a long time (2 years or more).

Around the third day after your baby is born, your milk will come in. Following a Caesarean section, however, or if you are anaemic, you may find this doesn't happen until the fourth, fifth or even sixth day. It may not be very politically correct to say so, but most men really like this part – even the most flat-chested women gain a cleavage! For some men, it can be difficult getting used to their partner's breasts – previously regarded as a major erogenous zone – being used for this very practical purpose (!) so a slight reaction to a new, fuller figure is only to be expected. Conversely, in the midst of the emotional, hormonal and physical changes already occurring at this time, many women tend to feel irritated by this reaction to their 'new' figure. Try not to let it become an issue for either of you.

Initially, when establishing breastfeeding, you will feel very uncomfortable when your breasts become full of milk. They will probably 'leak', making you feel damp (if not downright drenched!); sometimes women also experience a slight rise in temperature and symptoms similar to having a flu-like illness. At this point your baby can also be unsettled – finding it harder to 'fix' onto the breast because, as the skin stretches over the full breast, the nipple becomes flatter.

 Top Tip: When your milk first comes in, you are likely to experience some leakage and may also display symptoms similar to having a flu-like illness.

When he does 'fix', he will not have to suck as strongly as before, and will need to learn that a *gentle* suck rewards him with lots of milk – sometimes more than he can swallow! He may splutter a bit to start with but he'll soon get the hang of it.

Once he gets a taste for the milk (as opposed to colostrum) and recognises that 'full tummy feeling', he will go to the opposite extreme! He is likely to make a complete pig of himself, and eat so much he gives himself tummy ache, leading in turn to his crying a lot and being very restless. You'll probably also notice a change in the contents of his nappies, in colour, consistency and smell! Usually after 24 to 36 hours things will start to settle down to something approaching normality. Your baby will have grown more accustomed to milk and feeling full, and your body will have worked out how to produce a more appropriate quantity. After this initial influx, supply generally meets demand, and so it is unlikely that your breasts will feel quite so full again.

 Top Tip: *As days go by, your body will grow accustomed to producing the right amount of milk to meet demand and your baby will learn to drink enough without feeling too full.*

In the early days, many babies develop a blister on their top lip. This is referred to as a sucking blister and is caused by the lip gripping your nipple or a teat. This is not serious and causes baby no discomfort. They usually disappear very quickly (within hours) although they can appear after feeds on a regular basis.

But Is He Getting Enough?

Breastfeeding mums always worry about the amount of milk their babies are getting. If women had glass breasts – better still, calibrated at the side – many more would breastfeed! The trouble is, all newborn, breastfed babies behave differently –

101

they can feed as frequently as every 1–2 hours, or may go as long as 5–6 hours between feeds (occasionally even longer!). And like adults, babies don't eat the same amount at every meal. So try to relax – if your baby is content and sleeps well in between feeds, he is almost certainly getting enough.

 Top Tip: *Healthy babies do not starve themselves! And, just like adults, babies do not eat the same amount at every meal.*

Possible Problems When Breastfeeding
1. **Sore nipples**
- If your nipples get sore, it can be extremely uncomfortable with you feeling sure that junior has razor blades for gums! This is often due to poor positioning during feeding so ask your midwife to help you to position your baby correctly. You will soon recognise the sensation when baby is correctly positioned, and you will certainly know when it isn't quite right! It sounds daft, but a good tip is to aim your nipple at your baby's nose – this means he has to open his mouth wide to 'fix', and prevents him chewing (very painfully) on you!

 Top Tip: *The secret of 'pain-free' breastfeeding is correct positioning.*

- There are numerous nipple creams, lotions and potions on the market and some mums swear by them. They don't work for everyone, however – if you think about it logically, you need your nipples to toughen up, whereas most creams only soften them. Ask other new mums about what worked for them.

- One of the best remedies for sore nipples is to express a small amount of your breast milk onto the surface of your nipple, and then let it dry in the air.
- If you have sore nipples and want to give them a chance to heal and feel less tender, you can express your milk and give it to your baby in a (sterilised) medicine cup or eggcup. Unlike reverting to an occasional bottle, feeding this way means that the baby has to use the same technique (and facial muscles) as at the breast and will, therefore, find it easier to return to breastfeeding once you are. Many maternity units promote this as an alternative to offering occasional bottles to breastfed babies but, if no one has explained it to you and you want to know more, ask your midwife or health visitor for advice. Some babies cope well with the change of technique necessary to move between breast and bottle – and, as a result, their mums are normally quite happy about giving them the occasional bottle – but other babies seem confused by the switch. You'll soon discover which applies to your child.
- In many cases, expressing milk can ease the pain of sore nipples in the short term. For some women, however, a longer-term solution is to feed through a nipple shield (also known as a Mexican Hat) or even a bottle teat, both of which help lessen the impact of baby's gums on their nipples! Some experts, however, believe that this means that the baby has to work much harder, having to suck the milk from the breast into the teat and from the teat into his mouth. If a baby is especially small, was born early, or is jaundiced, they may find feeding like this more difficult. You might find that, if you suggest doing this as a course of action, some midwives and health visitors will be less than enthusiastic, but many mums confess to having used one of

these methods as lifesavers during the early days, several even saying they would have given up breastfeeding if they hadn't!

2. **Full breasts**
- If you have drunk lots of fluid, or rested well, you may find your breasts feel very full with baby showing no signs of waking. You may choose to express a small amount to ease the situation, but remember that 'supply meets demand', so if you express and then feed, next time you will make even more milk!
- Hot and cold flannels can help to relieve some of the discomfort.
- If you want to express milk from your breasts because you are going out, or want someone else to feed your baby, it is usually better to do it at the end of a feed, and only for a short time (for example 5–10 minutes). See below for the best way to store the milk.

3. **Mastitis**
   Whilst breastfeeding, it is not uncommon for women to develop mastitis. This is when an area of one breast (or, occasionally, both) becomes red, lumpy and sore. It will also be hot to the touch and you may feel feverish. Regularly examine your breasts and, if you notice an area that looks pink or red, or feels lumpier than normal, this may be a sign that a duct is becoming blocked. Gentle massage and ensuring the baby fixes well and regularly at the breast can alleviate the symptoms before full-blown mastitis occurs. However, should you feel generally unwell, often with an accompanied fever and a red, tender, hot spot, you probably have mastitis and will need to make an appointment to see your GP, who will prescribe antibiotics (which will change the colour of your poo).

Mastitis occurs when a milk duct becomes blocked, restricting the flow of milk. Symptoms can be relieved by putting hot flannels on the affected breast to encourage milk flow. An alternative cure, which seems to work for many people, is to put large raw cabbage leaves inside your bra, changing them as necessary until the symptoms ease.

Until relatively recently, women with mastitis were advised to stop feeding from the affected breast, but current theory now suggests that it is better to continue feeding because this gets the milk moving again! In the short term, this can be uncomfortable, but the relief afterwards is well worth it!

Some women will get mastitis several times while others breastfeed several children and never get it.

Top Tip: *Mastitis is not uncommon in breast-feeding women. It can often be relieved using 'natural' remedies but, in some cases, may require antibiotics.*

SAVING AND STORING BREAST MILK

If you are breastfeeding and want baby to be less dependent on you, you can express milk. This can be done by hand or using a hand or electric pump. If you're considering buying a pump, shop around. Do not be afraid to take them out of their boxes, because some of them are easier to work than others. Expressing by hand can be very effective, but a good technique takes time to learn and some people simply don't like doing it!

You can also collect drips from one breast whilst you are feeding on the other side. The easiest way to collect milk is by using 'Woolwich Shells'. These can be bought from your local pharmacist, relatively cheaply. You will need to sterilise them prior to use. They clip together and have a small spout to help you pour the milk from them. Always make sure the spout is at the top, otherwise you risk losing your precious milk, and getting wet into the bargain!

You can save breast milk in the fridge for up to 24 hours, after which time you need to freeze it. Once frozen, however, it will keep for up to three months. Always label milk in the freezer, either using a freezer pen or sticky label – you think you will remember how long it has been there, but you won't!

A good way to avoid having lots of expensive baby bottles in the freezer is to invest in a few old-fashioned, oblong ice cube trays from the market. Measure the capacity of a single cube – they are normally about 1 ounce or 30 mls. Cut up the ice cube tray, sterilise the individual plastic rectangles and then pour your milk in. Date the side of the cube with a marker pen, and place in a plastic bag in the freezer. The added bonus is that you can defrost the correct amount for each feed, rather than waste milk by defrosting more than you need.

Top Tip: Breast milk can be kept in the fridge for up to 24 hours but, if frozen, will keep for up to three months.

INCREASING YOUR MILK SUPPLY

Earlier, we saw how babies are subject to periodic growth spurts. If you are successfully breastfeeding and keen to keep up with your baby's particular growth spurts, it is good to have some strategies to increase milk quantity and flow for these times, for example:

- Always make sure your baby 'fixes' well during feeds. This means there is the best possible contact, which reduces the risk of sore nipples, but also causes maximum stimulation for you to produce milk.

- Increase your fluid intake (at least 3 litres per day), and eat a nutritious, well balanced diet (sufficient fruit, vegetables, carbohydrates and protein).
- Spend a couple of days concentrating on resting and feeding your baby. Leave the household chores to others, or leave them completely.
- Feed frequently. At least every 2–3 hours. Supply meets demand and this will stimulate your body to make more milk.
- Feed your baby for long enough to enable him to get the hind milk. (The first milk the baby takes at each feed is more thirst-quenching, with basic nutrients. After a while the fat content of the milk increases. This is referred to as the hind milk, and is particularly filling.)
- Feed your baby from both breasts at each feed.
- Learn relaxation techniques that will encourage the 'let down' reflex, thus increasing the flow of milk when baby sucks. Ask your midwife or health visitor about these.
- If you need to give 'top up' feeds, always offer them to baby after breastfeeding and only when *absolutely* necessary. The amount given and frequency of these top ups should diminish as your milk supply increases.

 Top Tip: There are things you can do to increase your milk supply. These include resting more, increasing your fluid intake, learning relaxation techniques and ensuring your baby fixes well and feeds frequently.

BUT YOU SAID YOU WANTED TO INCREASE YOUR MILK SUPPLY...

Bottle-feeding

If you have chosen to bottle-feed your baby, or find breast-feeding isn't right for you, ask for help during the initial feeds. Many new mums who aren't breastfeeding seem reluctant to ask for help but, especially if you've had little contact with small babies before, you are bound to need help and guidance.

> **Top Tip:** If you've decided to bottle-feed, don't be reluctant to ask for help because you're not breastfeeding. Seek advice on the best way to give your child what he needs.

Those parents who decide to bottle-feed need to choose the

formula to use for their baby. Once you've chosen it, try to stick to it. Do not be tempted to 'chop and change' formulae unless there is a really good reason – it's not good for your baby. And, as in the case of breastfed babies, don't expect the amount he takes at each feed, or the regularity of feeds, to stay the same – expect it to vary a bit.

There are numerous formula feeds available, and the one you choose is entirely up to you. They all contain nutrients suitable for babies, although the exact constituents do vary. Some may be more suited to larger, hungrier babies, others (like Wysoy, a soya milk) may be the formula of choice for those with a family history of allergies (although still less effective than breast milk).

Always make up your baby's feeds exactly according to the manufacturer's instructions. Never be tempted to add a little extra and, if you lose count of the scoops you have put in, discard the bottle and start again. In the same way, don't 'economise' by making the feed too weak – this will mean your baby gets a weak, unbalanced feed, which will leave him hungry.

 Top Tip: *Avoid the temptation to chop and change formulae and always follow the manufacturer's instructions exactly.*

In hospitals, ready-made feeds are usually available. These come in glass bottles with disposable teats (purely for convenience). They can be served at room temperature, although many babies prefer the feed to be warmed slightly. Cartons of ready-made feeds are available from chemists and supermarkets, but they work out expensive if you use them regularly. You also need to transfer the feed into a sterilised bottle before you use it.

Remember that a bottle-fed baby can be more prone to 'posetting' (bringing up a small amount of feed, usually accompanied by a burp); he may be more 'windy' and constipated than a breastfed baby. To help keep wind to a minimum, stop him sucking in air by keeping the milk level up in the bottle.

USING BOTTLES
General guidelines for using bottles:

- *Never* heat a baby's milk in the microwave. 'Hot spots' can occur within the liquid, meaning that although the general temperature may be satisfactory, there are areas that are much hotter than the rest. These can burn your baby's mouth.
- *Never* 'prop' feed. This involves sitting your baby in a baby seat with a cushion on his tummy and a bottle placed on top, angled so that he has the teat in his mouth. This is not a safe way to feed. If your baby chokes in this position, he has no means of either getting rid of the bottle or getting himself more upright.
- *Never* use unsterilised equipment. Even if you wash your baby's bottles and teats in a dishwasher, you will still need to sterilise all feeding equipment in the early days.
- *Always* follow the manufacturer's instructions exactly for sterilising (whether it is using sterilising tablets or liquid, steam or microwave sterilising). Taking shortcuts may leave bottles, teats, etc. not fully clean, increasing the chance of your baby becoming unwell.
- *Remember*, rubbing a small amount of salt in the teat prior to washing will loosen deposits of milk curds, and enable them to be easily removed by washing.

2. The Other End

There's no getting away from it – most of what goes in at one end comes out at the other! And you have to learn to deal with it. Newborn babies, especially breastfed ones, wee and poo a lot! Consequently, nappies don't tend to stay on for long before a change is needed so it's a good idea, initially at least, to buy the cheapest disposable nappies.

- If you have a baby boy, always make sure his penis is pointing down (towards his knees) when putting his nappy on. Do it any other way and you're likely to find that he has a dry nappy, but has soaked his clothes!
- Always have a wedge of cotton wool ready to place strategically as soon as you remove his nappy. Up until about the age of 11 weeks, baby boys have an instant 'reflex' which makes them wee as soon as their penis is uncovered. During one of her first outings with her son, one mum ventured into the changing room of a well-known children's store. Suitably impressed with the facilities, she laid her baby on a changing mat while another lady changed her six-month-old daughter on a second mat nearby. As soon as the mum removed her son's nappy, he peed straight over his head and soaked the little girl's dungarees, just as her mum was putting them back on!
- If you have a baby girl always clean her bottom by washing from front to back. This prevents bacteria from the anus (back passage) getting into the vagina.
- Always take care to clean any skin which has had urine or faeces on it – especially all the folds of skin.

The Colours of Poo

Lots of people ask 'So what exactly is normal?', so here's a guide!

★ The first motions passed by baby are black/dark green, and very sticky (often compared to tar). This is called meconium, and can last for a few days.

★ Once your milk comes in, your baby's poo will turn yellow (a bit like mustard pickle).

★ If you are breastfeeding, the shade of yellow will vary according to what you have been eating. If you eat an unusual food for you, be prepared to see the result in your baby's nappy the next day!

★ Bottle-fed babies tend to have harder, more formed poo than breastfed babies.

★ Green lumpy poo can mean your baby is over-feeding (difficult, as you cannot put a newborn baby on a diet!). Some babies also do this prior to a growth spurt.

★ Green watery poo can indicate your baby is under-feeding. This can happen if he is unwell, if your milk supply does not meet demand, or if mum is unwell. Babies like this are usually irritable because they feel hungry!

• New parents can be alarmed when seeing what appears to be blood in their newborn baby's nappy. The pinkish/reddish tinge on the nappy can be due to several things. Little girls occasionally have a sort of 'mini period', caused by an alteration in hormone levels following delivery. But, most commonly, it is caused by substances (urates) in the urine of every new baby which react with the chemicals in the stay-dry lining of the nappies. It causes the baby no

discomfort (but frightens the parents to death) and normally sorts itself out within hours. Of course, if in any doubt or if you're particularly concerned, show the nappy to your midwife or doctor.

- If you are using modern, super-duper nappies with ultra-absorbent linings, avoid using nappy cream. This is because creams can prevent the nappy lining from working effectively by keeping the urine in contact with the skin. In fact if you *do* use a cream, it may actually cause your baby's bottom to become sore. In the earliest days, however, some good, old-fashioned Vaseline, applied to the skin, can mean it is easier to wash the tar-like meconium off.

- Shop around to find the type of nappy that best suits your child and bear in mind that, as your baby grows, the nappy that worked well in the early days may no longer be as effective.

- If, despite your best efforts, your baby's bottom still becomes red and sore, don't get too stressed! It is not a reflection of your ability to care for your child! Small babies have very sensitive skin and some react very strongly to the ammonia in their urine. He may need to be changed more frequently, or need nappies that are more absorbent. On the other hand, he may need more fluid, so that his urine is less concentrated (especially if it is a very warm day). But it may simply be that his skin reacts to the creams or toiletries that you use, or even to the detergent you use to wash his nappies or clothes.

Top Tip: _In the early days, you'll be changing your baby's nappy a lot. It may be a good idea to buy cheaper nappies to start with._

3. Sleep - Yours and The Baby's

'_An alarm clock is an object used for waking up people who don't have kids._'

Anonymous

Sleep, or rather the lack of it, features largely in the first six weeks of parenthood. Most small babies seem almost nocturnal – they sleep a lot during the day, but are perky at night. Whatever you have heard – the child who sleeps through the night from day one really is incredibly rare (it's just that parents with older kids tend to have short memories about this kind of thing!).

Top Tip: _Sleep deprivation is one of the oldest forms of torture, but most children get the hang of it – in one form or another – eventually!_

Sleep-wise, the first six weeks is a difficult time for parents – you are trying to recover from the labour, get to grips with your new role (emotionally and physically) and keep the other parts of your life in balance too. Broken nights are the last thing you need and many new parents feel totally desperate for sleep; you can end up feeling so tired that you are sure you will die if you don't sleep soon! Additionally, if your baby was born early (particularly before 37 weeks) his sleep cycles are likely to be particularly erratic, due to the immaturity of his central nervous system.

Unfortunately, in most situations, there are no quick fixes – your baby has got to learn how to fall (and stay) asleep, just as he is learning many other things while he negotiates his way through his first weeks. For most parents, it's just a case of feeling their way, day by day, until they hit upon a means of coping.

There is some good news, though. Before the age of three months, your baby can't really learn any bad habits, so you can experiment with different ways of getting him off to sleep and discover which works best for you both. The list of options is endless, but could include feeding to sleep, rocking or holding him close, having a bath with him to tire him out, joining the 3 a.m. drivers' club or taking him for a walk in the buggy or pram. One dad discovered that if he made a cassette tape of a running tap for his son and played it, on a loop, throughout the night, his baby slept right through! (How he discovered this to be the case, however, we're not quite sure!) There are no hard and fast rules and you'll soon discover what does (or does not) suit you and your child. *The Parentalk Guide to Sleep* contains lots more information and advice about sleep throughout your child's early years.

 Top Tip: *In the early days your baby cannot pick up any 'bad' sleeping habits, so find out what works best for you and stick with it!*

Good Ideas for Sleep-filled Nights

Every baby is different, but there are some general rules that really can make a difference:

- *Be boring at night, but interesting during the day.* However tempting it may be, when he needs feeding at night try to avoid talking or playing with him. Once his bedtime has arrived, feed and change him during the night in subdued lighting and maintain a quiet, bland atmosphere (e.g. no radio or TV). This helps him to distinguish night from day very early on. Experts reckon that babies as young as four weeks are aware of light and dark cycles (called 'circadian rhythms').

- *If you have a partner, talk to one another about how you can help each other cope.* If one of you is working (usually, but not exclusively, dad) he will need to get some sleep at night in order to function. At weekends, however (or days off), maybe he can do a couple of night shifts with junior. Even with a breastfed baby, a bit of organisation means dad can give him previously expressed and stored breast milk. You'd be amazed at the difference a regular night (or two) of uninterrupted sleep can make! Other couples reach an agreement whereby one of them does the early shift every night (attending to the baby between, say, bedtime and 3 a.m.), while the other does the second shift (3 a.m. until 8 a.m.). However you cope, the important thing is to talk about it with each other. That way you'll avoid the feeling of resentment that you're doing the lion's share.

 Top Tip: *If possible, do a 'deal' with your partner to ensure that each of you gets one night of undisturbed sleep every week.*

- *Get other people involved.* If grandparents (or aunts and uncles) volunteer to have baby overnight – even just once – and you can cope with leaving him, take them up on the offer. You will feel much better for it!
- *Be kind to yourself.* When baby sleeps during the day, try to avoid the temptation to dash round cleaning the house, cooking, washing, etc. Instead, sit down, put your feet up, watch daytime TV, read a magazine, or a book on astrophysics (if that's your thing), but *rest*! Although many men and women prefer not to go to bed during the day, anything you can do to rest will make you feel much better. You need to recover – no one can cope indefinitely without sleep. Similarly, at weekends, make sure you both have a bit of 'time off'.
- *Follow the rules for 'safe' sleeping.* With eight babies dying

suddenly and unexpectedly each week in the UK, cot death must be one of any new parent's greatest fears. Following an immense amount of research, some clear guidelines have emerged for reducing the risk of Sudden Infant Death Syndrome (SIDS). As a direct result of the 'Back to Sleep' campaign, the incidence has dramatically reduced over the past few years. See Chapter 9 (Health Matters) for a more detailed look at this issue.

Top Tip: *Be realistic about your expectations regarding your baby's sleeping. The new baby who regularly sleeps through the night really is extremely rare.*

4. Cord Care

Many new parents do not like touching the remains of their baby's umbilical cord. When baby is born the cord is clamped with a plastic peg (in some cases, if the umbilical cord is particularly thick, two clamps may be used). Once your midwife is sure that the cord is beginning to dry out (usually around 36-48 hours following delivery), the clamp is removed. The remaining stump eventually shrivels and turns black, falling off completely after 5 to 10 days. It often smells unpleasant – sometimes making parents concerned – but this is, in fact, entirely normal.

Looking after your baby's cord can reduce the risk of infection, so even if you don't like touching it, try, at least, to keep it dry. There is no need to apply any cream or lotion to the stump, although sometimes a midwife or doctor will advise you to use surgical spirit or an antiseptic powder to clean it.

Alternatively, they may give you a special swab especially for the job. It is very important to clean the skin around the umbilicus and, if you think it looks red or swollen, sore or 'weepy', contact your doctor or midwife. Never pull the cord, or try to remove it – let it fall off in its own time.

 Top Tip: *Many parents dislike touching their baby's cord. At the very least, however, you should try and keep it dry. It will fall off after 5–10 days.*

---

5. Bath Time

It really does not matter when you bath your baby. There is no reason why you have to rush round in the morning, ensuring he is bathed, especially if you have to take another child to school. Similarly, many working dads seem to come into their own at bath time and so evening bathing may fit better into your lifestyle. There are really only two things to take into consideration when thinking about the best bath time for your baby:

1. **Before a feed is usually better than after**
    It makes sense really – you probably wouldn't choose to take a bath after a large meal either!

2. **Bathing followed by feeding often helps babies to sleep well**
    If your child is particularly unsettled at a certain time of the day it may be beneficial to adjust your routine with this in mind!

Bathing Regulations

Here are ten top tips for clean, happy babies (and clean, happy mums and dads!):

1. **Have everything you need nearby before you start**
    If you are worried about being disturbed, take the phone off the hook, or leave the answering machine to take calls!

2. **Remember that, until they get used to it, most young babies do not like bath time!**
    Young babies often feel insecure in the large, watery ocean of an adult bath. A cheap way to make the baby feel safer is to bath him in a kitchen sink, or washing-up bowl. In comparison, specially designed baby baths can be awkward to handle and heavy when full, especially if you're trying to manoeuvre one having just had a Caesarean section – save your money!

3. **Try increasing your baby's confidence by gently 'bouncing' him in the water**
    Bouncing your baby in the water – or letting him kick against the side of the bowl, bath or sink – helps to give him a sense of stability and lets him know he is in a safe place. Most babies also seem calmer in the bath if someone is holding and supporting them, rather than simply being laid on a cut-out baby bath sponge (although these are still invaluable, particularly if you have more than one baby). If you use a sponge, and your baby seems unhappy in the bath, try supporting him instead – there may be a big improvement.

4. **Babies love having baths with mum or dad so, even from an early age, do it as often as you can**
    Initially, this may be a two-person operation, with one of

you in the bath and the other handing him in and then taking him out again to dry him. Likewise an older brother or sister will love sharing a bath with the new arrival. Regardless of who's in the tub, it can be a great way of spending a bit of quality time together.

5. **Always check the temperature of the water carefully**
There are thermometers available from most chemists and childcare shops which can help but, for most people, the much cheaper option of testing the water with their elbow, or wrist, gives just as good an idea of whether the water is too hot, cold or just right! In practice, so determined are they to avoid scalding, that many new parents tend to go to the other extreme, making the water too cool. Like most adults, small babies don't like being immersed in lukewarm water, so without making it too hot, make the water comfortably warm. Trust your elbow!

6. **You do not need to spend a fortune on baby bath products**
Basic, fragrance-free, gentle products are best. Baby bath may make your baby easier to handle than baby oil (although all wet babies tend to be a bit slippery!) and smothering him in powder can dry his skin so it's probably best avoided early on. If, on the other hand, your baby was overdue, or has dry skin, a few drops of oil in the bath will help to moisturise it. Some babies also develop dry, scaly scalps – known as 'cradle cap'. It doesn't look very attractive, but it's not serious and will not cause your baby undue distress; it can be treated by rubbing a little olive oil into your baby's scalp and leaving it there for a few hours. Then, using a baby comb, you should be able to loosen the dry patches. Once done, wash his hair as normal. If the problem persists, however, consult your GP or health visitor.

121

7. **When bathing or 'topping and tailing' a baby, avoid contact with his eyes, unless they appear sticky**
Newborn babies often have 'glued-up' eyes – they are particularly prone to mild infections because of the blood and liquid they came into contact with during delivery. If his eyes do become stuck – normally with yellow gunk – gently wipe them with cotton wool that has been soaked in cooled boiled water. Only use each piece of cotton wool once, always wiping from the inside (by his nose) outwards. Never use the same piece of cotton wool for both eyes, as this will spread the infection. Repeat this at each feed for 24 hours and, if the condition does not seem to be improving, contact your GP or midwife. If ever the discharge from your baby's eyes appears green, do as before, but also make an appointment to see your GP – it may take mild antibiotic eye drops to clear it up.

8. **Use separate plastic bowls for 'topping and tailing' a baby**
You can buy special 'top and tail' bowls for washing your

baby but, in truth, two plastic bowls will do just as good a job. If you can find different colours, all the better, because you can ensure that you always use one colour for his bottom and the other for his face.

9. **Don't be worried by the appearance of small white spots on your baby's face**
Mums and dads are sometimes worried by the appearance of these small white spots, but this is rarely serious. Seen on almost all new babies, these are called *melia*, and are caused by hormonal changes following delivery. They disappear within a few days of delivery without treatment. Try to leave them alone, even if some of them look red, but if they burst and weep fluid, clean them with cool boiled water. If they persist or appear to spread, consult your GP.

10. **Always keep safety in mind**
Never leave your baby unattended in the bath – even for a moment. Similarly, mop up spillages as soon as possible – it is easy to forget they occurred and slip whilst holding your baby. And make sure that he is always safe and secure while you're getting the bath ready. It all sounds obvious, but you'd be surprised what people do! One student midwife working in Special Care nearly had a fit when a mum left her tiny, pre-term baby *on top* of the incubator, while she went to fill the bath with water. This tiny baby was about 5 ft off the ground, lying on a perspex roof! The midwife says that she has never moved so fast in all her life!

 Top Tip: *Once they get into the swing of it, most babies love bath time. It may just take a while for them to get used to the idea!*

---

6. Crying

Before he develops other means to tell you what he wants or how he feels, crying is your baby's only method of communication! Be prepared – some babies are more vocal than others! Others may cry, at varying volume, for no apparent reason.

Many first-time parents are surprised by quite how much (and how often) babies cry. In 1965 a study looking at 80 newborn babies found that, on average, they cried for 1.75 hours per day during the second week of life, increasing to 2.75 at six weeks. Further research (in the US) has since confirmed these findings – suggesting that babies cry for about two hours a day during the first few weeks and reach a peak of three hours a day by six weeks. Fortunately, they don't put in a two-hour crying stint all at once(!) and the amount they cry normally subsides by three months of age, and then remains constant from that point until they are about a year old.

Contrary to popular belief:

- First babies do not tend to cry more than subsequent children.
- Breastfed babies do not cry more than bottle-fed babies (research in 1989 showed there was no significant difference between the two groups).
- If you have a baby that is breastfed and cries a lot, changing to bottle-feeding is unlikely to result in him crying less.

Additionally, there are several distinctly different ways of crying – some start with a whimper and gradually build to a crescendo, others start at 200 decibels and stay there!

Top Tip: *Crying is your baby's only means of communication during the first few weeks of life – he can't even smile (unless accompanied by wind!) before six weeks old!*

As time goes by, you will quickly learn to recognise your own child's cry and get to know what different cries mean. In the meantime, whenever your baby cries, run through the following checklist, asking yourself:

1. Does he need changing?
2. Does he need feeding?
3. Is he hot/cold?
4. Is he uncomfortable?
5. Is he in pain (i.e. drawing up knees, colicky, 'windy', vomiting, etc.)?

Learning to distinguish one cry from another is a bit of an art, but you'll be surprised how quickly you'll pick it up and learn what your child does and doesn't like. For instance, some babies will wait whilst you change them prior to a feed, others want to be fed, and want it *now*!!! Some babies do not mind having a dirty nappy, others will cry as soon as their nappy needs changing.

In the vast majority of cases, you'll find yourself able to detect why your baby is crying at any particular time and deal with it. General tips for helping to soothe a crying baby include:

- Talking to him in a calm, soft, quiet way (no matter how irritated you feel!).
- Picking him up and cuddling him.
- Placing a warm hand on his stomach or chest.

- Rocking him in your arms.
- Walking with him, either in your arms, in a buggy, or a baby sling.
- Putting him near 'household noises' – many children like the noise of a vacuum cleaner, or washing machine.
- Putting him in his car seat and taking him for a drive.

As a general rule, most newborns like sensations similar to those they were used to in the womb, which is why background noises (hums), rocking and walking tend to be big favourites. Additionally, a distressed child will normally respond better to being handled confidently, preferably by someone with warm hands!

Handling a crying baby in a public place is a challenge for any parent – as someone once remarked, 'Why *do* parents take their children to supermarkets to cry?!'

And as your baby lets rip in a crowded lift, it's tempting to believe that he is much worse behaved than everyone else's! So if he seems more unsettled, unhappy, or difficult than others you meet, it's good to remember that:

- Other people's babies will often *seem* better behaved than yours (it carries on into childhood and right through the teenage years too!).
- You only see other children for a very short time, and very few babies are good *all* the time.
- Your own baby's crying will always upset you more than the sobs of other people's and so will seem more intrusive.
- Babies have personalities too! Some babies are far more laid back than others, but they'll probably make up for lost time later on!
- Babies can be affected by the behaviour, attitude and emotional health of their mum and/or dad – if you're upset, stressed or unwell it may influence the amount your baby cries.

7. Going Out with Your Baby

Kate decided to take her two-week-old into town for a first trip out. She packed up the car, drove to the car park, waited for a space, took a ticket and, thinking ahead, parked strategically at the end of a row of cars. This would mean she was able to open all the car doors and easily get Ellie out of her car seat.

Then Kate opened the boot and spent the next 40 minutes trying to assemble the pram. Realising she was on a losing streak she decided to ring James (her husband) at the office. His secretary explained he was out of the office at a meeting all afternoon – had he not mentioned it?

Eventually, after another 15–20 minutes battling with the pram, she frustratedly got back in the car, paid £1.00 for the parking space (after hunting around to find the right coins for the ticket machine), and drove home. Just in time for the next feed!

 Top Tip: *Make sure you know how your car seat, pram, etc. work before setting out.*

You'll soon discover, if you haven't already, that early outings require the organisation of a military operation, so go easy on yourself and don't expect to rush anywhere to start with! If you're going shopping, don't be too ambitious about the amount you will be able to do on any one trip or the time you will be able to achieve it in!

 Top Tip: *Set realistic goals for your first trips out. Don't take too much on.*

In the same way, think about the most appropriate equipment to take with you for your journey. Try to make life as easy as possible for yourself. If you are driving into town, for example, and only have a few things to buy, a car seat and sling might be more useful than a buggy or pram. Likewise, a buggy may be a pain to use for a bus, tube or train journey, but, when carrying lots of shopping around, a sling may only prove successful in bringing on an aching back!

Get to know (from friends, other mums and dads, or local information offices) where baby-changing facilities are situated – anyone with children will soon tell you which are the best! This will save hours of trudging around with the 'sweet smell of nappy' wafting up your nose, looking for somewhere suitable! Bear in mind that, although less common nowadays, some changing facilities are situated only in ladies' toilets – not so great for the men, or for feeding in!

Whenever you go out, don't forget to take a drink and snack for yourself. Particularly if you are a breastfeeding mum, you'll often suddenly become very hungry and thirsty.

If you are visiting friends who have children, don't take everything except the kitchen sink with you. There is a commonly accepted but unwritten rule that states that all parents help each other – so make the most of it! And why not keep some nappies and a basic change of clothes at anyone's house you regularly visit. Keeping an extra change in your car could also help you out in an emergency.

 Top Tip: Keep a few 'baby essentials' at the homes of friends and relations whom you regularly visit.

'And Stretch, Two, Three, Four . . .'

Looking After Yourself

With all this attention being paid to the new addition it's easy to forget about looking after yourself and your partner. The fact is, however, that a vital part of looking after your baby *is* looking after yourself, so don't miss out. Remember to give yourself an emotional and physical health check from time to time.

For obvious reasons, this chapter focuses mainly on helping mum back to full fitness. That doesn't mean, however, that any dads reading this book should merely skip the next few pages! Quite the opposite. There are plenty of things that *you* can do to help to speed your partner's recovery. If nothing else, show her that she is supported by someone who is, at least, aware of the things that new mums have to face!

Top Tip: *A vital part of looking after your baby is looking after yourself, so make sure that you're getting enough time to recover from the birth and recharge your batteries.*

Mum's Postnatal Recovery

You don't have to have a degree in midwifery to realise that, as well as being incredibly rewarding, labour and birth is an exhausting business. As a new mum, whether you've had a vaginal delivery or a Caesarean section, it takes time to recover – the majority of which you'll be doing at home. So be kind to yourself, don't try and take on the world too quickly! If you have had a Caesarean section, it is estimated that it takes between three and six months to fully regain your previous energy, so you will need to take extra care. If you can, enlist extra help in the early days to ensure you make a complete and speedy recovery.

Now stre-e-e-etch and . . . relax!

Many hospitals and community midwives will give you lots of information leaflets to take home, all of which will provide tips for ensuring as quick a recovery as possible.

One of these leaflets will give you advice on 'postnatal exercise'. For those of us who get out of breath running a bath, never mind running a marathon, this sheet is probably the one most likely to end up 'filed' in the bin! But don't worry, it doesn't recommend a full aerobic workout, so dig it out and read it! In it you should find basic, common-sense exercises that will strengthen the muscles that have been stretched to capacity by pregnancy, and help you to regain your figure. Bear in mind, however, that though these exercises are very effective, they won't help you get a body fit for *Baywatch* if you only had a body fit for *Crimewatch* to start with! For dads, too, a bit of exercise probably won't go amiss so why not encourage your partner to get back to full fitness by doing the exercises with her?

Even if you don't reach the point of donning your tracksuit and trainers, as you recover from the birth do make sure that you do your *pelvic floor* exercises. During your pregnancy, your midwife will have told you how important these are. They involve the tightening and relaxing of the muscles around your front passage (the ones you would use if you suddenly needed – midstream – to stop yourself urinating). Make sure you do them regularly and frequently. It really will make a difference and is much better than the alternative – embarrassing incontinence when you sneeze or cough in later years. Pelvic floor exercises really are important and have the additional benefit of being easy to do anytime and anywhere! You can even do them while you're sitting here reading this book! You may be concerned at how little muscle control you have in the early days, but you'll also be surprised how quickly the muscle tone returns once you establish a regular pelvic floor 'workout'!

Top Tip: Pelvic floor exercises are extremely important for new mums. Don't forget to do them!

Come On Then – Honestly, How Do I Look?
Pregnancy affects every part of a woman's body – changes in your hair (texture and growth rate) and skin colour are common. Once your baby has arrived, however, you will begin to see things start returning to normal.

131

- *Hair.* In the first weeks of motherhood, you may experience significant hair loss. During pregnancy, your hair – which normally grows in a cycle of loss and regrowth – just carries on growing with little, if any, falling out. As a result, some women find that their hair never looked better, whilst, for others, it becomes thick and unmanageable. Following the birth, all this excess hair begins to fall out – sometimes quite dramatically! It can be a shock to see your locks in the sink after washing, or big clumps coming out when you brush your hair, but don't worry. Your normal hair growth pattern of loss and regrowth will re-establish itself once your hormone levels settle down.

IT SAYS HERE PREGNANCY CAUSES HAIR LOSS. HOW MANY BABIES HAVE YOU HAD, DAD!

- *Skin colour.* Some women experience a darkening of their skin during pregnancy, particularly on their face. Known as 'chloasma', this usually occurs around the forehead, nose, mouth and chin. You may also find that you tan more easily, and it lasts for longer, though it tends to be uneven. Other common changes include the skin around moles, birthmarks and freckles becoming darker and, in some cases, the appearance of a dark line on your stomach, from your pubic bone to your tummy button (known as *linea nigra*). Once again, as your hormone levels settle down, your skin will usually return to its pre-pregnant colour, but keep an eye on any moles that also seem to be changing and report them to your GP.

- *Stretch marks.* These normally appear in the latter stages of pregnancy, on your abdomen, back and breasts. They can become very red and may itch. Stretch marks can be the cause of much consternation for new mums but, despite a proliferation of creams and lotions on the market, there is not much you can do, either to stop them appearing or to get rid of them. After delivery, any marks will stop itching and gradually turn a silvery colour. All the darkened areas of skin will fade, although the *linea nigra* can remain a very faint line for a long time after baby's birth.

 Top Tip: *Pregnancy affects every part of a woman's body and each will take time to return to its pre-pregnancy state.*

Making It Look Easy

In previous chapters we've looked at ways of making your recovery easier. Making sure that you're getting enough sleep, that you're supported by friends and family, and ensuring that you don't over-exert yourself, is half the battle. Here, however, are a few extra tips, gleaned from other parents, that may also help in getting you back on your feet and feeling fit (they are especially relevant if you have had a Caesarean section):

- *Rest and sleep.* For minimal disturbance at night you may choose to have a Moses basket (or similar) next to your bed. If your home is on more than one floor, it may also be handy to have a pram (or similar) downstairs for your baby to sleep in during the day, as this will reduce your trips up and down stairs.

- *Feeding.* Whether feeding by breast or bottle, try to make yourself as comfortable as possible while doing so. Make sure you are well supported as you sit – perhaps with a cushion in the small of your back – and on a chair that is a good height for you. Bear in mind that some 'nursing chairs' are very low for women who have had abdominal surgery. You may also find it helpful to have one, or both, knees bent – dangling feet will only pull on your tummy muscles. In this situation, an upside-down washing-up bowl can act as a good footrest. Additionally, some women also like to place a pillow across their lap while breastfeeding – it raises their baby slightly but also protects a Caesarean wound.

- *Toddlers and older children.* It is advisable to avoid lifting any heavy weight – including small children – for at least three weeks following a Caesarean section. Lifting heavy items is normally fairly easy to avoid but, if you're already a parent, not lifting children can be extremely difficult (if not impossible) in practice. It's entirely understandable, with the arrival of a new baby, that your existing children will want more cuddles and more of your attention than before. In this adjustment period, the last thing you'll want to do is exclude them, but you also need to take care of yourself. One solution is to sit down and encourage your toddler to cuddle up next to you on the sofa, chair or bed. This way they don't feel excluded and can have as many cuddles as before, but without the strain of you lifting them up. Similarly, if you have a small child who still needs to be lifted into a high chair, picnic meals on a plastic tablecloth on the floor might prove a good short-term solution!

Use other people as much as possible to help with general lifting, but if it really is unavoidable, always remember to bend your knees not your back.

- *Driving.* Again, this is only an issue if you've had a Caesarean – you will be advised not to drive for six weeks following this abdominal surgery. Insurers used to specify that you weren't allowed to drive following any general anaesthetic but, now that many women have a spinal or epidural anaesthetic instead for their sections, the guidelines are less clear. The main thing is to be confident, before getting back behind the wheel, that you would be able to do a (painless) emergency stop. It may also be a good idea to check with your own insurance company about whether they impose any special rules and regulations. Be prepared to feel nervous and shaky behind the wheel initially.

   One mum decided to drive herself to her local super-market on her own. She didn't need much shopping but, with a poor local bus service, she was eager to get back behind the wheel. She got there, parked, did the shopping, had a coffee in the snack bar, and rang her partner to come and pick her up! She couldn't face the prospect of manoeuvring out of the parking space and then driving home, even though it was only a couple of miles!

   For many women, getting back behind the wheel means the welcome return of some independence. But as the mum above can testify, however desperate you are to get driving again, make sure you really are ready!

- *Sex.* How soon you resume your sex life following the birth is entirely a personal decision and varies considerably between couples. Most will wait until a Caesarean wound has healed and any vaginal bleeding has stopped, but the most common approach is to wait until after the six-week postnatal check. See Chapter 11 for more detail concerning sex and contraception.

- *Antenatal complications.* If your pregnancy was complicated by an additional health problem, or you have a long-standing medical condition, you may need to take specific measures to ensure you recover well. Seek advice from your midwife and doctor. If you were prescribed any medication during your pregnancy, it is important that you consult your doctor before you stop taking it.

Top Tip: *How quickly you resume your 'before baby' activities will vary tremendously. Take things at your own pace and do not feel pressurised into doing more than you feel you can.*

You Are What You Eat – The Importance of a Good Diet

A major factor in ensuring the ongoing health and wellbeing of your family is diet. Having a new baby provides you with a fantastic opportunity to eat healthily. We're not talking about the latest 'Z-plan' diet, or any other weight-reduction regime for that matter – just eating more fresh fruit and vegetables, fish, etc. and cutting down on the 'junk'. It makes sense really – the better you eat, the better you'll feel and the better you'll be up to caring for your new baby. Additionally, of course, if you decide with someone else (partner, friend, etc.) to change your diet for the better, there is the added advantage that you'll be able to spur each other on through weaker moments!

Healthy eating makes good sense. Eating well gives you more

energy whilst maintaining your weight at a healthy level, it improves your mental alertness and concentration span, as well as ensuring that you feel physically and emotionally better.

 Top Tip: *Becoming a parent provides a great opportunity to start looking after yourself and a healthy diet is a good place to start.*

If you are anaemic, or lost a lot of blood at delivery, you may be advised to increase your iron intake. Oral iron supplements are readily available but can have the unfortunate side-effects of either constipation or diarrhoea! A more natural method is simply to increase the iron content of your diet by eating dried fruits, leafy green vegetables and sardines. If it takes your fancy, you can even have the *occasional* Guinness!

Diet while Breastfeeding

If you are breastfeeding, diet is more important than ever because you really are eating for two! Eating well will provide your body with all the nutrients necessary for your full recovery as well as meeting the needs of your growing baby. You should eat plenty of protein and calcium, which are found in foods like fish, meat, eggs and dairy products. Vegetarians can also find these constituents in pulses and wholegrains.

Some of the weight gained during pregnancy is fat, which has been laid down specifically in readiness for breastfeeding. Once breastfeeding is fully established, your baby will take around 1,000 calories a day and you'll actually need to increase your own food intake. For this reason, it is not advisable to go on a reduced calorie diet while breastfeeding. You will probably feel hungrier than normal and should avoid skipping meals, although you may find smaller, more frequent meals suit you better than three square meals a day.

The occasional 'food sin' is only to be expected – after all you're only human – but, on the whole, make sure snacks are nutritious. Try to avoid *always* reaching for the crisps, biscuits, chocolate bars or other instantly available food! Eat fruit instead, which is just as instantly available, and things like sandwiches, baked potatoes and pasta. Many breastfeeding women find that they do lose weight simply by eating healthily.

 Top Tip: *It's not a good idea to go on a reduced calorie diet while breastfeeding.*

Breastfeeding also makes you thirsty so reach for water and fruit juices, rather than sugary fizzy drinks. Milkshakes are also a healthy source of calcium, although some parents say that their babies appear more colicky if mum has drunk a lot of milk.

Foods to Avoid while Breastfeeding

You've probably already heard one or two 'old wives' tales' about foods to avoid whilst breastfeeding. Certain foods are, they say, 'guaranteed' to upset your baby, keep him awake, give him wind or change the consistency of his nappy contents. Common culprits range from onions and oranges to garlic and curry (and other rich or spicy foods). There is probably an element of truth in all these things, but it is also true that different babies like and dislike different things. After all, Indian babies' mothers eat curries all the time, with no adverse effects!

Any food you eat does not pass directly into your breast milk – it is first digested by you – but some particularly rich or spicy foods *will* alter the taste of your milk because they are acidic. If your baby doesn't like the new taste, he may object! Consequently, introduce any new, highly spiced, or slightly unusual foods individually, so that if your baby does have an upset stomach you can easily identify the cause.

 Top Tip: *Plan for a mid-feed attack of the munchies by having a nutritious snack easily available. Avoid slipping into a Mars-Bar-a-day habit!*

'Oh Baby, I Got the Blues' – Baby Blues and Postnatal Depression

Having felt totally euphoric immediately after delivery most new mothers feel tearful around the third day following delivery, often referred to as the 'baby blues'. This is due to a combination of altering hormone levels, feeling physically sore and uncomfortable from delivery, and the daunting responsibility of parenthood. During pregnancy our society treats women as very special, yet as soon as baby is born he becomes the centre of attention, with many visitors not sparing as much thought for the mum. This can be hard to adjust to.

 Top Tip: *Most women suffer the baby blues at around the third day after delivery. They usually subside on their own within a short space of time.*

Additionally, about 1 in 10 women will suffer with more severe postnatal depression. This lasts for a longer period of time

139

than the baby blues, and results in you feeling irritable, tired, weepy and often strangely distanced from your child. Women with postnatal depression also complain of an inability to concentrate, feeling confused and experiencing feelings of inadequacy – in terms of caring for their baby, but also in other relationships. They can also suffer with insomnia, loss of appetite, and changes in bowel habit.

The reasons why women suffer postnatal depression are varied and little understood. However, research shows that women are more prone to postnatal depression if they have just given birth to their first child, have a history of suffering pre-menstrual depression, or were depressed at any point during their pregnancy.

The early symptoms of depression are usually first noticed by others, but it is not uncommon for the sufferer to deny vehemently that there is a problem. This is completely understandable – you're likely to be very frightened by the emotions you feel. The important thing to remember is that no one is immune from this condition – depression is no respecter of persons. It is no reflection upon you as a person or on your ability as a mother.

If, as a dad, you suspect that your partner may be suffering from postnatal depression, or if, as a new mum, you suspect that you may be dipping into depression yourself, talk to your midwife, health visitor or GP as soon as possible. The symptoms can diminish after a few weeks, but if they persist you should get help. Correct medication and/or counselling can help you get through it. Remember – it's a common problem, there *is* help available and there's no reason why you should suffer alone.

Top Tip: *If you think you, or your partner, may be suffering from postnatal depression, seek professional help from your GP, midwife or health visitor. Depression sometimes resolves itself, but can also be effectively treated by a combination of counselling, medication and rest.*

Keeping Your Relationship Healthy

A baby is a real test for any relationship so, in the midst of all this adjustment to new roles and responsibilities, it's vital that you also give some attention to your relationship with your partner.

It's a stressful time for you both: mum recovering from the birth, allowing her body and emotions to settle down and (especially if she's breastfeeding) trying to get to grips with her new role; dad trying to look after mum and any existing children, whilst also carrying out all his usual responsibilities. It's very easy for men to end up feeling left out at this time. They have loads of jobs to do, which perhaps have previously not been their responsibility, whilst the woman they love appears totally wrapped up in this new demanding individual.

Top Tip: *It's only reasonable for your baby to be your main focus, but don't let your other relationships fall into disrepair as a result.*

It's all too easy to find yourselves with no time for each other. You long for your child to sleep, so you can snatch a bit of time together, only to be disappointed when neither of you can

141

keep your eyes open long enough to sustain a conversation! In any case, often the last thing you'll feel like doing at the end of a busy day, once junior has finally gone to sleep, is talking about anything! It's easier to flop in front of the TV and switch off. The problem is, if you're not careful, this lack of quality time together will provide the perfect seedbed for misunderstanding and resentment to grow. So even though it may take a gargantuan effort to switch the TV off and concentrate, it is absolutely vital that you do it. You need to engage with one another's worlds and find out what is going on there. Just a few minutes, here and there, to find out how your partner is doing and what they are feeling will make all the difference.

If you can get someone to look after the baby on a regular basis (even if it is only once a month), even better! Go out together – even if it's only for an hour – and have a chat. Enjoy each other's company and celebrate the fact that you're facing this exciting challenge together.

 Top Tip: Contented couples usually end up with better adjusted children and 'easier' babies, so make time for one another.

You may be amazed to discover that a little light relief will also help you reconnect with your sense of humour! Talk together, laugh together and learn to forgive one another – it's the essence of a good relationship. Give each other time to adjust – to new responsibilities, new pressures and this new little person who has become part of your lives. Not everyone moves at the same pace, so try, occasionally, to give each other the benefit of the doubt.

Of course there will sometimes be crisis points – they are inevitable and everyone has them. But working hard at your relationship – by committing yourselves to communicating with one another and being willing to forgive one another's slip-ups and blind spots – will make you better prepared for the crises when they do hit. Make it a habit – talk, listen, talk, listen and then talk and listen some more!

 Top Tip: Work hard at finding time for your relationship – talk, listen, talk, listen and then talk and listen some more!

Caution: Men at Work

For new dads in full-time employment, the first six weeks can be particularly pressurised. After all, when you become a dad, you're taking on a second job. The pressure which comes from being pulled in two or more directions at once is stressful and exhausting. It may take a while to find your own solution to the 'conflict' between the expectations of your new family and your existing job. The main problem is that it seems to be a 'no-win' situation – you feel guilty for not being at home when you have to work and you worry about work when you're at home.

In the early days, many men struggle to get to work on time. This may be because they have been up half the night, because they hung on for one more glimpse, or because their partner needed them to help with the morning chaos that tends to ensue in every house with children!

But research also shows that men tend to work harder and longer hours when their first child is born and then longer still on the arrival of their second. The jury is out as to why this is – it could be the 'hunter gatherer' instinct kicking in, a defence mechanism used to avoid what is happening at home, or some other reason – but, whatever the cause, it's not a great situation. Like it or not, your partner and baby need you.

'Work-life balance', as it has become known, will probably always be an issue, never completely resolved. But now is your chance to make a decision about how you're going to live your life. It's tempting to believe that, one day, we will all be sufficiently established in our work to have the freedom to spend more time with the kids. The reality, however, is that unless we get into the habit of spending time with our children from their very earliest days, when we do finally find ourselves with some time to spare, they won't be interested in spending it with us. A child's first years aren't called the formative years for nothing! The experiences that we have in these earliest, and most fleeting, of days help to shape who we are. So even during this first six weeks, do what you can to juggle work and home. Talk to your employer and see if there is any flexibility in working arrangements – there may be more than you think there is. Where you have choices, be determined to choose the course of action which will most benefit your new family. The two most obvious areas to do this in are working late and out of hours, work-related, socialising.

1. **Working late**

   We all have to work late sometimes – the pressure's on, something needs finishing, a crisis has occurred. Fine. If you need to work late, work late. But what about those times when you don't really *need* to work late but have just become accustomed to doing so? The odd half an hour here, hour there – it's almost a habit. This is when it's worth telling yourself to simply *go home*. Working late is an ever-increasing part of our culture in the UK, but many successful businessmen and captains of industry have reached positions of influence without compromising their

144

role as fathers. And in any case, at the end of the day, which is really the most important?

2. **Work-related, out of hours, socialising**
   Another tricky one. No one's suggesting that you should cut out all of your work social life – it's often an important part of working in a team and many a deal is struck over a drink after work – but certainly in the first weeks and months, keep such engagements to a minimum. On the vast majority of occasions, make a point of going home!

 Top Tip: *Keep an eye on your 'work-life balance'. It's never easy, but keep checking where your priorities really lie. As a general rule, unless you genuinely have to work late, it is probably best to go home!*

Men Not at Work

Families who have no employment face particular challenges in the first weeks of parenthood. Men can feel inadequate and depressed at their lack of prospects in the light of the new addition to their family. Women whose partners are not working can also feel the pressure of the lack of financial security that unemployment brings, with their feelings of vulnerability heightened by their inability to contribute because of the new baby. Society does not always help. Women speak of worrying for their partners when well-intentioned (perhaps?) relatives and friends have passed comments like 'Will you get a job now?'

If you find yourself in this situation, the most important

thing is to talk to each other about your concerns and your feelings. It will help you get things into perspective. Secondly, ensure that you are claiming all the appropriate benefits while you look for work. Thirdly, check that you are getting the best possible help for finding employment. Your local employment office should be able to help you.

Top Tip: Unhelpful comments may well come your way at this time – ignore them as best you can. Make sure that you are receiving all the benefits you're entitled to.

'The Doctor Will See You Now . . .'

Baby Health Matters

Almost universally when it comes to health, new parents find an unexpected item has been added to their already long list of responsibilities – the role of 'Chief Worrier'! In the early days, when he is unable to clearly communicate, every cough, sneeze, runny nappy, solid nappy, burp and fluctuation in temperature will have you scuttling to the medical dictionary! It's no exaggeration to say that many a parent has rushed their baby to accident and emergency only to be told, 'It's wind, love, nothing to worry about!' It's reassuring really – a small child needs to have someone looking out for him – but you might as well prepare yourself for the fact that this is now a full-time occupation! The chances are – for one reason or another – you will worry about your kids for the rest of your life!

Some parents, knowing they are likely to be immersed in the medical needs of their children for some years to come, enrol in a basic first aid course before their baby arrives. It's a great idea. Knowing what to do in an emergency, be it major or minor, will increase your confidence and help you deal with the situation more calmly and appropriately. Both the St John's Ambulance and the Red Cross offer excellent first aid courses and their numbers will be in your local phone book.

 Top Tip: *'Chief Worrier' appears on every parent's job description!*

Routine Health Checks

- *At, or soon after, delivery*, all babies have initial health checks carried out by midwives and doctors. If your baby remains well, he may not be examined again until you are at home. Your GP may well do a brief examination when they first meet your baby.
- *At seven days old*, all babies in the UK have a 'Guthrie test'. Your baby has a blood sample taken (from a stab on his heel) which is collected on a special card and sent away for analysis. It is a screening test for *phenylketonuria*, a rare metabolic disorder that causes severe developmental problems if untreated but, when treated, means children develop perfectly normally. Depending on your local Health Authority policy, thyroid function may also be assessed in this test. Again this condition is rare, and early treatment prevents long-term health problems.
- *At around 10 days*, your health visitor takes over your care, although midwives still retain professional responsibility

for mother and baby until 28 days after delivery. Initially your health visitor may visit you at home to weigh your baby, check he is doing well, and deal with any of your questions.

After the initial visit your health visitor will encourage you to take your baby to the local baby clinic to be weighed regularly. This is a good opportunity to raise any issues worrying you and meet other parents with small children. It can be amazingly reassuring that other people's children are exactly the same as yours! This may not be an issue in the first six weeks, but it certainly is as time goes by! Many long-lasting friendships start at the local baby clinic! These are the people you will stand outside playgroup and primary school with, for years to come!

- *At six weeks*, the next developmental check happens, undertaken either by your GP or a doctor at your local Child Health Clinic. You will automatically be sent an appointment for this. Mum will also have a postnatal check-up at around this time. Most commonly this is done by your GP, but if you have had a difficult pregnancy or delivery you may be asked to return to the hospital for this appointment.

 Top Tip: Your baby will undergo several routine examinations during the early part of his life. If you are, in any way, worried about any aspect of your child's health, contact your GP, health visitor or midwife.

Common Health Issues

Jaundice

Many new babies develop jaundice soon after birth. There are various types of jaundice, but the one we normally associate with newborn babies is known as *physiological jaundice*. Time for a quick biology lesson here: physiological jaundice is caused by the breakdown of foetal haemoglobin (HbF), which, while a baby is in the womb, is carried in lots of small red blood cells. Once a baby is born, his blood begins to change and he starts making adult haemoglobin (HbA), which contains fewer, larger red blood cells. The baby's system then tries to break down all the old small red blood cells he no longer needs before discharging them from his body (in his urine). This process can take time, partly due to the immaturity of the baby's liver. So a baby converts what he can and stores what he can't cope with in a safe place, away from all his vital organs, just under the skin. It is this that produces the yellow tinge to the skin that we recognise as jaundice.

Most babies who develop jaundice show no sign of illness and, within a few days, with regular feeds, the excess passes out from the body in the urine. Jaundice can take longer to fade in breastfed babies than their bottle-fed counterparts and, for all babies, the yellow tinge often lingers for a while in the whites of the eyes.

Frequent, regular feeds and ultraviolet light help speed up the breakdown of the cells and the subsequent time it takes to get rid of them. So if your baby looks yellow, don't be surprised if your midwife or doctor suggests putting him in the sunlight (if we ever get any!).

If your baby appears drowsy, reluctant to feed, or if your midwife is at all concerned, she may take a sample of your baby's blood (again from a stab on his heel), just to make sure that he is dealing with jaundice effectively.

Controlling his Temperature

New babies are not very good at controlling their temperature and so it falls to you to make sure that he becomes neither too hot nor too cold. Maternity wards often feel like summer in the tropics and so, unsurprisingly, when they leave hospital most new parents worry about keeping their baby warm. In fact, many babies are more at risk from becoming too hot. You don't need to keep your home at the temperature of your average Mediterranean villa – between 16 and 20°C is ideal. A room thermometer for his bedroom may be a good investment. Additionally, a good general rule for babies is, day or night, they need one more layer than you're wearing.

Your baby's hands and feet are always cooler than the rest of his body, so to get a truer idea of his temperature, feel his head, chest, or the back of his neck. If he is cool, it's better to add a layer of clothing than turn up the heating because these can be easily removed if he begins to overheat. The Foundation for the Study of Sudden Infant Deaths (FSID) has produced a list of the tog value of clothes likely to be used for a baby and, cumulatively, they should not exceed eight. Copies of this list are commonly available in maternity units, libraries or from the FSID (address at the back of the book).

RISES IN YOUR BABY'S TEMPERATURE

A baby's body temperature, just like an adult's, is prone to some fluctuation – it doesn't *always* mean that he is ill. However, if your baby's temperature rises above normal, it is important to look out for other symptoms that may indicate your baby is unwell. Changes in his behaviour, for example – not feeding, a darkening of his urine, a change in his poo colour and/or consistency, general lethargy, etc. – may all add to your suspicions that he is coming down with something. Short-term things that you can do are:

- Take off his clothes to help cool him down.
- Sponge over his body with tepid water and leave his skin to dry in the air.
- Offer him cooled-down boiled water to drink – if he is dehydrated (and therefore thirsty) he will drink it.

However, if you are at all worried, if his temperature is very high, or if his symptoms persist, never hesitate to call your doctor, midwife, health visitor or NHS Direct. Most health care professionals apply two golden rules:

- Always listen to concerned parents. Great importance is placed on parental instinct – mum or dad really do know best!
- Always take any concerns over young babies very seriously.

If in doubt *always* call – you'll never be sorry that you did.

 Top Tip: If you're worried about a rising temperature, always call your doctor – you'll never be sorry that you did.

Wind

Winding during and after feeds is vital for many babies, especially those who are bottle-fed. Some babies, however they are fed, are more prone to wind than others – and boys more so than girls – but if you usually breastfeed, but give occasional bottles, the chances are your baby will be more 'windy' following the bottle feed.

One way of combating wind is to wind him regularly throughout the feed. With bottle-fed babies, make sure that the bottle is always at an angle ensuring the teat is full of milk. This also prevents baby gulping too much air.

You'll discover the best way to wind your own baby with practice. Some babies find it easier to bring up wind sitting up while you gently rub their back; others prefer to be held against your shoulder. It won't take long before you know what your child prefers.

Colic

Colic is a spasmodic pain in the abdomen. It is more common in boys than girls and is often characterised by high-pitched screaming, with a baby clenching his fists and drawing his knees up to his tummy. For some reason, colic most commonly occurs in the evening. Unfortunately, though there are colicky babies all over the world, no one yet really knows the cause or the definitive treatment.

If your baby has colic, your natural reaction is to pick him up and rock him, changing position frequently as his crying

153

persists. However, the most recent research indicates that babies with colic tend to settle more quickly when they are handled less and rocked less. So if you haven't tried it yet, let your baby have a rest in his cot for a short while (say, about ten minutes) – less stimulation may work well for him.

Even though colic can drive many a mum and dad to distraction – playing havoc with your confidence because your baby seems inconsolable – there is no evidence that it damages your baby in any way. It's often just a matter of sitting it out until he grows out of it (which he will, commonly, by about four months of age).

Top Tip: Colic does more harm to the parent – frazzling their nerves and lowering their confidence – than it does to the baby. For him, there are no known adverse effects!

Other tips for coping with colic:

- Play monotonous sounds – like a hairdryer, hoover or washing machine. This can help your baby become less alert to his surroundings and less irritable as a result. Music may also work for him.
- Although the 'handle him less' advice is the most up to date, some babies do seem to be helped by gentle, rhythmical movements. Does he enjoy being in a sling, for example, or pushed in the pram?
- Give him skin to skin contact when you do pick him up – babies love this sensation and the sound of your heartbeat can have a reassuring, calming effect.
- Ask your pharmacist about gripe water and colic drops (which you give your baby prior to a feed) that may help.

- Some babies find relief sitting in their car seat in front of the washing machine or tumble drier. This combines a slightly more upright position with no handling, with a monotonous noise and even something to watch if there is a bright item in the machine. We're not suggesting your baby spends *all* his time in front of the washing machine, but you may find it helps sometimes!

If you are concerned, or need further advice, talk to your health visitor or GP.

To Dummy or Not to Dummy, That Is the Question

If ever there was a contentious issue it has to be – the dummy! Some suggest that, if a baby suffers with wind or colic, it can be helped if he's given a dummy because the sucking action helps to alleviate the pain. Some parents view dummies, or soothers, as lifesavers (and their inventor as a deserving nominee for the Nobel Peace Prize), others see them as a necessary evil, whilst a large number of mums and dads detest them completely – branding them 'unhygienic' and a way of 'storing up trouble for the future'.

One grandmother had always claimed that there was 'no place for those horrible things in any child's life' until, that is, she met her grandson! He had terrible wind during the first few weeks and in the end it was actually the granny who suggested trying him with a dummy!

It's totally up to you which way you jump, but make sure it's *your* decision! If you do decide to use dummies, however, always sterilise them prior to use. Don't be tempted to lick them yourself, or wipe them on a handkerchief before giving them to your baby! And replace them every few weeks, or earlier if the rubber appears worn.

Note: Some dummy designs incorporate a small compartment for holding liquid. Even if you have one of these, avoid putting juice in it – even the 'baby-friendly' juices contain sweeteners and can cause gum and teeth problems later on in life.

Top Tip: *Not everyone likes the idea of a dummy but, for some, it is a real winner! Go for the approach that you feel most comfortable with.*

Sneezing and Blocked Noses

Babies often sneeze a fair bit – this is normal and rarely anything to be concerned about. It's just a case of their sensitive little noses becoming acclimatised to all the microscopic particles in the air that we are already used to.

Similarly, if your baby appears to have a blocked nose, don't worry too much. Young babies are 'nose breathers' and can snuffle away without really experiencing any discomfort. Some children are 'snufflier' than others but, even so, there is no need to try and make them sneeze. Parents have even been known to poke rolled up pieces of tissue into their baby's nostril in an attempt to start him sneezing, but this is never a good idea. At this early stage, allergies are extremely unusual (especially in breastfed babies), but still not unheard of. Is there anything new around that your baby might be allergic to?

If your baby's bunged up nose seems to hamper his feeding, talk to your GP, health visitor, midwife or pharmacist. Likewise consult them if his blocked nose persists for more than a few days, or is associated with other symptoms. Your local chemist will stock a range of remedies, but rather than just buying them off the shelf, talk to your pharmacist first. If they can't help they might suggest you see your GP with a view to getting some nasal drops on prescription.

And one last piece of advice – if, at any time, your baby seems to be having trouble breathing, if it appears laborious, or if he looks pale, greyish, or bluish, go to Casualty immediately.

Rashes

New babies often have rashes, usually caused by their skin simply getting used to all the things we have already built up an immunity to. Very innocuous things can cause a rash – a change in washing powder, or a new (i.e. as yet unwashed) fabric. As a general rule, it's a good idea to wash all your baby's clothes before he starts wearing them. The good news is that these rashes usually disappear as quickly as they appear and shouldn't normally be a cause for concern.

If, however, a rash is accompanied by a change in baby's behaviour (not wanting to feed, general unhappiness and/or irritability), seek prompt medical advice. Partly due to a great deal of recent media coverage, at the earliest sign of a rash, a lot of parents' first reaction is 'meningitis!'. The quickest way to test for the possibility of a meningitis rash is to use the *tumbler test* (see Meningitis, below).

Top Tip: *Minor rashes are very common in newborn babies. Always consult a professional if in doubt. To test for the possibility of a meningitis rash, use the tumbler test.*

Sudden Infant Death Syndrome: Reducing the Risk

One of the biggest fears that every new parent faces is that their baby will suddenly stop breathing in the night. Babies who die completely unexpectedly, for no apparent reason, are described as having suffered Sudden Infant Death Syndrome (SIDS), also known as Cot Death. Even though research by FSID has shown that, tragically, an average of eight babies die per week in the UK as a result of SIDS, statistically it is not common. The most likely age for it to occur, however, is between two and three months and every parent will want to do everything within their power to prevent it.

A lot of time, money and energy have been put into researching the causes of SIDS. It might not stop you worrying, but there are five important steps you can take to provide as much protection as possible for your baby.

1. **Back to sleep and feet to foot**
   Unless your midwife or doctor gives you a specific reason not to, always *put your baby to sleep lying on his back*. His feet should also be touching the bottom of the cot or Moses basket so that he can't wriggle further down the bed and end up with the blankets covering his head. In the same way, because they can easily slip over his head, duvets and quilts aren't regarded as safe for babies under a year, and pillows aren't safe until he's two years old. Additionally, always use cotton blankets that you can tuck in and never put a hat on your baby to sleep in even if he is cold.

2. **Smoke free zone**
   There is a proven link between Cot Death and smoking. Research suggests that the number of deaths from SIDS would be reduced by almost two-thirds if parents didn't smoke. So the best advice is to quit now! But if you simply can't give up:

- Always smoke well away from your baby (never in the same room).
- Ensure all visitors do the same.
- Cut down the number of cigarettes you smoke to the bare minimum.
- Make sure you get some good support if you're trying to cut down or stop smoking. See the back of the book for details of the NHS Smoking Quitline.

3. Not too hot
Don't let your baby get too hot. Once out of the, often exceptionally hot, hospital environment, let him adjust to the normal temperatures of your home. Try and get a feel for how hot or cold he becomes during the night (see the section on your baby's temperature, above).

4. Prompt medical advice
If your baby is unwell, especially with a raised temperature, breathing difficulties, or is less responsive than normal, see a doctor promptly. You know your child better than anyone else and if your intuition is telling you something isn't right, listen and act on it.

5. Bed sharing for comfort, not to sleep
Some studies show that bed sharing is beneficial to a baby's health, others link it with SIDS. There is no definitive view. The latest Department of Health advice errs on the side of caution – they recognise that many parents do share a bed with their baby, especially to feed or to give him comfort, but they recommend that you put him back into his own cot or Moses basket to sleep.

One conclusion of the research which is clear, however, is that you should never share your bed with your baby if you:

- have drunk alcohol;
- smoke (even if you don't actually smoke in bed);
- are taking any medicines or drugs that make you drowsy;
- are feeling excessively tired.

If you choose to have your baby in bed with you (and many parents do), be aware of the following advice:

- Make sure your partner knows your baby is in the bed.
- Make sure your baby is away from your pillows, the duvet or bedclothes, and not likely to roll off the bed!
- Remember that, when sleeping in the family bed, your baby has a warm parent's body (or two) nearby. Don't overdress him so that he overheats.

ADDITIONAL ADVICE

There have been various other research projects, many funded by the Foundation for the Study of Infant Deaths, that suggest the risk can be reduced further by other simple measures, for example:

- Never let your baby sleep on a water bed or bean bag.
- Always use a firm, well-fitting mattress.
- Avoid placing cot bumpers, duvets, pillows and soft toys in your baby's cot.
- Always tuck your baby in firmly.

APNOEA ALARMS

There are a growing number of baby monitors on the market. The latest trend is to have an apnoea alarm – a mat on which your baby lies while he sleeps. If he stops breathing for more than a specific amount of time an alarm goes off. In a healthy child with no family history of SIDS, some may argue that the anxiety involved in listening for the alarm to go off can outweigh the benefits. In fact, studies conducted by the Foundation for the Study of Infant Deaths (see their details at the back of the book for more information) have found no evidence that monitors help to prevent cot death. You may choose to use an apnoea alarm if it makes you worry less, but never let it lull you into a false sense of security by making you less vigilant.

Top Tip: *Follow the five steps for reducing the chances of sudden infant death syndrome:*

- *Back to sleep and feet to foot*
- *Smoke free zone*
- *Not too hot*
- *Prompt medical advice*
- *Bed sharing for comfort, not sleep.*

Meningitis

Meningitis has had a very high profile over the last few years and, unsurprisingly, this has led to parents being keen to know how to spot it. Meningitis is an inflammation of the lining surrounding the brain and spinal chord and can be caused by either bacteria (bacterial meningitis) or viruses (viral meningitis). In babies, the symptoms are:

- fever, with hands and feet feeling cold
- refusing feeds or vomiting
- high pitched, 'moaning' cry
- a dislike of being handled, fretful
- neck retraction with arching of back

161

- a blank and staring expression
- difficult to wake, lethargic
- pale, blotchy complexion.

Some bacteria that cause meningitis can also cause septicaemia (blood poisoning) which causes a rash to appear under the skin as a cluster of tiny 'pin prick' spots. Roll a clear tumbler over the rash – if it blanches (fades) as you roll the glass, it is unlikely to be meningitis. If it does not blanch, but remains present, you must seek medical aid *immediately*.

If you suspect meningitis, contact your doctor *straight away*. Describe the symptoms carefully and explain that you suspect meningitis. If a doctor is not available, take your baby straight to your nearest Accident and Emergency Department. Do not wait for the rash – it may be the last symptom to appear and, in some cases, it may not appear at all.

For more information on meningitis and septicaemia, contact the Meningitis Trust (details at the back of the book) by calling their 24-hour helpline on 0845 6000 800.

Top Tip: Get to know the symptoms of meningitis. If you suspect it, get help straight away.

General Health Issues

Other People's Illnesses

Though it's obviously not a good idea to expose baby, or yourself, unnecessarily, if someone you know has a mildly infectious illness (like a cold, for example), it does not necessarily mean you have to avoid them completely. It's probably not a great idea to have them cuddle and kiss your child, but being in the same room needn't cause any problem. Babies receive immunity from the placenta, which lasts up until around three months of age. Breastfeeding, especially colostrum, further boosts this immunity, so even if you only fed your baby for a few days, you will have passed on some immunity to the diseases around us.

Safety First
Always take care to ensure the ongoing safety of your new baby. For example:

- Never hold a hot drink whilst carrying your baby – it is very easy to spill it when he wriggles.
- Never leave him unattended on a raised surface, such as a sofa or a bed – even for a moment.
- Never shake your baby. The brain is a large heavy structure on a stalk and shaking causes it to knock against the hard protective surface of the skull that surrounds it. This can obviously cause serious, long-term damage.

When to Call the Doctor
Just about every new parent must have, at one time or another, faced the dilemma of 'Should I call the doctor, or an ambulance, or am I worrying over nothing?' It's never an easy call to make – doctors, health visitors, midwives and nurses are busy people after all. However, even if you take nothing else away from the rest of this chapter, take this:

If you're in any doubt at all, call!

New babies are vulnerable little things and any professional will prefer to preside over a 'false alarm' than have you risk the health of your baby in the hope that everything's OK.

Top Tip: *If you're in any doubt, call the doctor. Trust your instinct.*

Immunisations

Although it doesn't strictly fit within the first six weeks, it's highly likely that, during this time, you will be beginning to think about what you'd like to do to protect your baby from disease. Many stories circulate in the press about the pros and cons of immunisation and it's therefore very easy to feel confused by the conflicting messages. Here's a rough guide:

- Babies at risk of *tuberculosis* may be immunised with BCG at birth, or at least within the first eight weeks of life.
- All mothers who have had *hepatitis B* during pregnancy, or are chronic hepatitis B carriers, should have their babies vaccinated against this illness at birth. Your doctors will advise you.
- *HIV positive* mothers will need to take special precautions to limit the chances of transfer of this disease to their baby at or after birth. Improved medication regimens are being developed all the time; your local clinicians will advise you and arrange follow-up for you and baby.
- *Polio, diphtheria, tetanus (known as the 'triple' vaccine), whooping cough, haemophilus influenza type B (meningitis).* All children in the UK should be vaccinated against these diseases. Usually the first injection is at around two months of age, and there are two follow-up injections at four-weekly intervals following the first. The aim is that all children should have received this first course of

164

injections, and consequently be protected from these potentially dangerous conditions, by six months of age.

Top Tip: Most children suffer minor illnesses throughout their entire childhood. Small children can appear to become unwell quickly, but also recover quickly. So don't panic! Take sensible, common sense precautions, but if junior does not appear to be improving, contact NHS Direct, your GP, health visitor or midwife.

Something for the Men

Thriving on Fatherhood

There are two problems with writing a chapter specially for men in a book like this. First, it can be an open invitation for men not to read the rest of the book and, second, it can leave the authors open to allegations of stereotyping – after all, not all men are disinterested fathers who won't read anything about parenting unless it is specifically directed at them. The truth is, however, even taking these problems into account, that most fathers, or fathers-to-be, do not read books about parenting – they leave it to their partners. But even in these days of anonymous sperm donation, men are, at the very least, jointly responsible for the creation of every foetus. So the main message of this chapter should be – make sure you read the rest of the book: it applies just as much to dads as it does to mums. That said, this chapter provides an opportunity to take a brief look at some specific issues which are particularly relevant to men as they get to grips with some of the responsibilities of parenthood, but which have not been covered elsewhere in the book.

Making the Most of Becoming a Dad

1. Look forward to fatherhood

- As you prepare for fatherhood, you may have mixed feelings. Am I ready? Am I mature enough? Can we afford it? All this is perfectly normal – no one can ever be completely prepared. And the truth is, it's OK to make mistakes – every mum and dad make them. If you're ready to give it a go, however, you'll learn as you go along and you'll discover your own way of 'doing' fatherhood.

167

- Recognise that fatherhood may be the most important job you'll ever have – your child is your legacy. Becoming a father is an incredible privilege. It won't always be easy for either you or your baby, but the rewards of working hard at being a dad are incredible.

- Use the opportunity to think about your life. Get ready for an adjustment. Evaluate your life goals and priorities and talk about them with someone, preferably your partner. It may not be something you're used to doing, but it will make a massive difference. For instance, what sort of dad do you want to be? Are there things that you're worried about? If you do not live with the mother of your child, what kind of role would you like to play in your child's life?

- Remember that babies and children always benefit from being looked after by their fathers – and, of course, it's a two-way street! You have a vital role to play. Take the initiative – try to lose the idea that one of you will be a 'primary' and the other a 'secondary' carer. Remind yourself that many dads say that, by taking their parental responsibilities seriously from day one and by working hard at forging a healthy, active relationship with their child, they themselves immediately reap the benefits. They discover a good life balance. They often do better in their jobs than less involved fathers and, as a result, feel a lot better in themselves too.

 Top Tip: Babies benefit from being looked after by their dads – and it's great for the dads too!

---

2. Prepare yourself as best you can
- Decide whether you're going to be present at the birth – most, but not all, dads are (see pages 25–6).

- Familiarise yourself with what labour entails and what you and your partner can expect. Not all antenatal classes are father-friendly, but in some areas they are more geared up for working with couples. In any case, if at all possible, go with your partner to all antenatal appointments – ask for times you can make. If you feel sidelined at any time, say so; remember, this is your child too.

- Remember that the better informed you are, the more able you will be to support your partner through her labour and beyond. This will make things easier on all of you – you, your partner and your baby. Talk with your partner about what you would both ideally want from the birth – and write it in a birth plan (see pages 22–5).

- Find out about all the financial welfare benefits available to you and your family.

- Try to avoid the temptation to over-stretch yourself financially. There are lots of hidden costs associated with becoming a parent that you may not fully appreciate until you are facing the bill. As much as you possibly can, make sure that you're not already struggling with debt re-payments before you start.

- Check out your parental rights. If you are not married, you're at a real disadvantage unless you apply for Parental Responsibility (which will give you the same rights as a married father). The fact that you and your partner are expecting a baby may mean you are already considering getting married but, at the very least, you should consider ensuring that your name is on the birth certificate (also see the section on registering your baby's birth in Chapter 11). You can obtain information about applying for Parental Responsibility by calling the Principal Registry's Children Section on 020 7947 6936. Application forms also can be downloaded from www.courtservice.gov.uk/fandl/forms/c(pra).pdf

- Check out your money rights. If you don't live with the mother of your child, and regardless of how much contact you expect to have with your child, you will have to pay Child Support. Contact the Child Support Agency (see the address at the back of the book) or make a private agreement with your baby's mother as to the amount you'll pay. Some fathers, eager to do the 'right' thing, massively over-stretch the amount they offer to pay and find themselves in financial problems, so be realistic about what you can and can't afford. Don't make payments in cash – you'll need to be able to provide proof of payment if asked.
- Talk to your employer about working arrangements surrounding the birth (also see page 41). If you have any choice in the matter, don't take on new big projects close to when the baby is due. Check out your paternity rights and give your boss plenty of notice about how you intend to play it.

 Top Tip: *You'll never have every angle covered, but making some preparations will help to take the stress out of early fatherhood.*

---

3. The birth
- Don't panic when contractions start or when her waters break – your partner will need you to be strong for her. If you're concerned, make a list beforehand of the things you'll need to do and when you'll need to do them. Remember an average labour is 12–16 hours long!
- Help your partner relax by encouraging her with her breathing, massaging her back and by using other re-laxation techniques.
- When labour begins in earnest, knowing already what your

partner wants will help you to support her better. If she's having difficulties, it may be down to you to speak on her behalf.

- Like it or not, labour is a messy business. Looking after yourself before and during the birth (getting enough sleep, eating enough, etc.) will help, but you may still feel shocked by the experience.

WHAT IF I MISS THE BIRTH?

Many dads are present at the birth of their child. Some fathers, however, through no choice of their own, miss it. Working abroad or away from home (particularly in the armed services) can leave new dads with little chance of getting to the birth, but some dads just get stuck in traffic nightmares, train delays, or a myriad of other things.

If you desperately wanted, and fully expected, to be at the birth of your child, but just couldn't make it in time, you'll understandably be pretty fed up. You may even wonder whether it will have any sort of long-term impact on your relationship with your partner or your ability to bond with your new baby. True, it might take a bit of time to work through with your partner – she will probably have wanted you to be there even more than you did yourself. That said, however, there's no reason why it should have any longer-term implications for your relationship with your child. It's just a matter of making sure that you get stuck in when you do get there!

 Top Tip: *Plan for what you will do when your partner's contractions start. Support your partner by familiarising yourself with what you can expect during labour.*

4. Early days

In the early hours, days and weeks:

- Get involved straight away. Don't wait to be asked by your partner or the midwives and doctors. You may feel under-prepared, clumsy even, but if you get stuck in you will be surprised how quickly you learn the skills you need. Many fathers talk about a confidence and enjoyment that they would never have imagined was possible before. You may be amazed to discover that the more you do, the more rewarding you'll find it.

- Work with your partner. Remember the maternal instinct can be extremely powerful and, in the early days, your partner may appear reluctant to share the baby – even with you. Give her a bit of time, but don't retreat and try not to be oversensitive about it. Gently suggest to your partner that she, your baby and you will all do better if you share the load. Don't give in to your own insecurities about handling your baby and let it become a reason for you to step away from being involved.

- Talk to your partner. As a couple, this is a vital part of ensuring that you can give your best to your child. Even if you don't live together, you and your partner are in this together, each with specific responsibilities. Talking to each other will help both of you to avoid feeling isolated and create a far more positive environment for your child's healthy development.

- Support your partner in her choice of feeding method (see page 97). If she chooses to breastfeed, encourage her to persevere – it will get easier. You may feel a bit of a 'spare part' to begin with, unable to take an active part in much of your baby's feeding. Remember, however, that you can still bath him, wind him, change him and settle him and, on occasion, it may also be possible for you to bottle-feed him with expressed breast milk. Resist the temptation to suggest switching away from breastfeeding to allow you to bottle-feed – you'll be able to feed him solids soon enough.

- If you have to go home leaving your baby and partner in hospital, come back as often as you can. Very occasionally, hospitals provide beds for new fathers, but this is quite rare.
- Once at home, give your partner real breaks. Spending time alone with your new baby will also help build your confidence and enjoyment in your role as a dad.
- Establish yourself as the one who, habitually, puts your baby to bed. This can be a special time and, because you won't smell of milk, you're likely to have more success than mum.
- Find out about the symptoms of postnatal depression. It's more than likely that you will be the one who first notices the need for expert help if your partner suffers in this way (see pages 139–40).
- If you have a car, don't always be the one who does the driving. Sit in the back occasionally, next to your baby, and enjoy being with him.
- Don't let sex become an issue. For a variety of reasons – sometimes physical, sometimes emotional – your partner may not be ready for full penetrative sex until some time after a new baby. Give yourselves a bit of time to adjust. Trying to force her into something that she's not ready for will only have a detrimental impact on your relationship. If she doesn't feel ready, focus instead on different types of intimacy. You may discover that just talking, cuddling and kissing brings an unexpected tenderness to your relationship.
- After your paternity leave has ended, instead of working harder, work less. Don't avoid the responsibilities of fatherhood by concentrating on those of employment. If you can make adjustments within your job – without compromising it – in order to gain more time, do so. And be determined to get home when you say you will.

- If your partner no longer wants to remain in a relationship with you, but wants you to play an active role in parenting your child, you will both need to work hard at discovering what works in your particular situation. Be prepared to try a variety of arrangements as you learn – it will take lots of patience, but it's worth it.
- Be prepared to encounter, and work at overcoming, the 'Dads are less important than mums' culture. Though attitudes are shifting for the better, changing facilities in women's toilets and visitors and professionals directing questions about baby care only to mums (and questions about sport only to dads) are all still a day-to-day reality. Be an informed, involved dad who breaks the mould.

Top Tip: *The rewards of fatherhood are incredible, so be an involved dad – from day one.*

Back to Life, Back to Reality

Getting On with Life

So now you're approaching the end of your first six weeks as a parent – you're almost a veteran! Looking back, it may even be difficult to remember what life was like without your baby on the scene! You'll be astonished at how quickly time has flown and amazed at how much has happened since your baby was born just 42 days ago! By now, you should also be feeling more confident about your role as a mum or dad and finding that you're doing things more instinctively than before. With every day that you continue to negotiate the challenges of parenthood, you'll discover little tricks for making life easier all round. Some you'll pick up from other people; many you'll discover for yourself; and some your baby will 'tell' you, by the way he responds to what you do.

'He Just Said His First Sentence!' - Development by Six Weeks

All babies change immensely in the first six weeks. You may not notice it at the time – after all you're watching him every day – but, looking back, you'll be amazed at the difference 42 days can make! While you're busy getting to grips with new parenthood, it's easy to let these changes slip by unnoticed, so take lots of photos and video. Label and date all photos – you'll be surprised how remarkably similar subsequent children can look, especially if you pass clothes down from one child to the next!

As you see your baby growing and changing, it's only natural to wonder whether he is doing 'OK' as far as his development is concerned. All babies develop at different rates. Some sit up and crawl early on, some don't; some sleep well from day one, others don't; the list is endless. Every parent wants the best for their baby, but try not to become too preoccupied with what he can and can't do. Avoid becoming embroiled in the 'competitive parent syndrome', where proud parents score points off one another in an attempt to claim the (imaginary) title of 'most advanced child'. Your child will develop at a speed that suits him and there's little you can do about it. Some things he'll learn quickly; others will take longer to get the hang of.

 Top Tip: *Try not to get sucked in to becoming a 'competitive parent'. All babies develop at different rates; the ones who are slower at learning one thing may well be quicker at learning another.*

That said, for a general idea of how your baby's development is progressing, keep an eye out for signs of any of the following as you reach the end of the first six weeks:

- The first signs of your baby's personality emerging. He will be getting used to life in your family, and become much more responsive.
- He may still cry a fair amount but he will be more responsive to your attempts to placate him. He will have a longer period awake during the day and will also demonstrate more control over his limbs – enjoying kicking his legs.
- Some babies may even be able to lift their heads momentarily while lying on their fronts, but will still not be able to do this when sitting.
- Your baby will be able to recognise and respond to you and your partner. This is a magical thing for any parent to experience for the first time. Your baby will turn his head when he hears your voice and will also stare at your face – even smiling at you – as you talk to him.

If you're concerned about any area of your baby's development, his six-week check will help to highlight whether there are any potential problems to keep an eye on.

Registering your Baby's Birth

It is an easy thing to forget in the busyness of early parenthood but by the end of the first six weeks you should have registered the birth of your baby. In England, Wales and Northern Ireland it is a *legal requirement* that you do so within 40 days of the birth. In Scotland, it must be done within three weeks.

- The midwife who delivered your baby, or was present if a doctor carried out the delivery, will have completed a birth notification form. This is a legal requirement for every midwife.
- If, for whatever reason, you had your baby in a different

geographical area from your usual place of residence – because you chose to, were visiting friends, were on business or holiday, or if you were transferred to another hospital for specialist care – you will have to return to that area to register the birth.

- Check if you need to make an appointment to register the birth. Some Registry Offices have a 'turn up any time' policy, but not all. There is no fee for registration.
- Important: If you are not married to your partner, only the mother's name can be put on your baby's birth certificate unless the father is also present to register the birth. Also see page 169 for information on Parental Responsibility for fathers.
- Choose a name. If necessary, you can change it later, but there may be a charge for it.
- Once his birth has been registered, your baby will be allocated a National Health Service number and you can start claiming child benefit for him. Claim as soon as you can – if you delay, you may lose benefit. Get a claim pack from your local Social Security Office, ring the Child Benefit Centre on 08701 555540 or click onto www.dss.gov.uk/lifeevent/benefits/childbenefit.htm.
- Many maternity units give you an information leaflet before you leave hospital that explains the procedure in your area, but if you have unanswered questions, ask your midwife or health visitor.

 Top Tip: *It is your legal responsibility to register your baby's birth. Don't leave it to the last minute!*

Getting Back into the Swing

Looking back, many parents talk about the first six weeks as being about the hardest period of early parenthood. Sure, life as a mum or dad is always going to be full of surprises – ask the parent of any teenager – but the first few weeks probably provide the steepest learning curve as new parents grapple with the unique challenges that every brand new baby brings.

You'll probably notice things getting a bit easier as the weeks pass and, before you know it, you'll be emerging, blinking at the light, from your 'new parent cocoon', ready to face the world again. And as you do so, it's only common sense to continue to stick to the good habits that you've developed in preparation for, and during, the first six weeks. They will help to make the transition easier.

Make Time for Yourself

Keep in Shape and Eat Healthily

Not only will you feel better – both physically and emotionally – you'll also be better able to look after your child as he grows up. Cut out eating between meals as often as you can, and eat a balanced diet including plenty of fruit and fresh vegetables. Find a form of exercise that you enjoy. Better still, find a friend who will go with you – it will toughen your resolve to stick at it! Remember that you don't have to spend a fortune joining a trendy gym (unless you really want to). Check out your local leisure centre first – many have very good facilities, for a fraction of the price, and no joining fee. They will also provide trained fitness experts who can help you assess your fitness and plan a realistic programme for you. Swimming is a good form of gentle exercise, too, and, if you want to do something

less formal, remember that walking is also very good for you –
you can even take your baby along!

Give Yourself Childcare Breaks to Help you De-stress

These needn't be very long – a regular couple of child-free hours
can make a big difference, especially in the middle of a hard
week. Make the most of friends and relatives who would jump
at the chance of spending an hour or two cooing over your
baby. Knowing that there's a regular time you can really call
your own will reduce your stress levels, helping you enjoy more
the time you do spend with your child.

Have a 'Proper' Night Out Occasionally and Spoil Yourself

There will inevitably be times when even the most devoted
parent resents the inhibitions a baby brings. A good antidote is
to have a proper night out (or even a night away, if you're very
organised) occasionally. It requires planning: babysitters,
bottles and breast pads may all feature! But none of the
planning will be wasted – you'll feel much better for it.

Make Time for Your Relationship

Enjoy Being Parents Together

Parenthood is a fantastic privilege. Appreciate one another and
make the most of every opportunity to be together with your
child.

Save Time for Each Other

Plan to spend time together away from the kids. Even if it's
only an hour a week, arrange for someone to take your baby
off your hands – put it in your diary in indelible ink! If

babysitters are a problem, make sure you at least spend some proper time together once your baby is in bed. Get a video and a bottle of wine, take the phone off the hook, and . . . you get the idea!

Talk and Listen to Each Other, Even When You Don't Feel Like It
Make time to talk on a regular basis. Switch off the TV or, at least, quit your TV-dinner habit. Encourage conversation instead, giving each other the opportunity to talk about the type of day you've had.

Surprise Your Partner by Showing Them Your Romantic Side!
It needn't be costly, but an unexpected gesture can mean a lot (and not just to women, men like it too!).

Don't Let Sex Become a Major Issue
Give each other time to get used to the idea of intimacy again. Some women take longer to recover, emotionally and physically, from birth and may need a bit of space. Some men are traumatised by the delivery and find the thought of sex difficult. Exhaustion can mean a lowering (or absence) of sex drive for either of you. It's at these times that it's good to remind yourself that the people who have the best sex lives are probably the ones whose partners get the most sleep! Before you both feel ready, it is important that you think about contraception. Many GPs will ask you about this when they first visit you at home following delivery, so it is a good idea to have thought about it before they ask the question!

- Breastfeeding is *not* a reliable form of contraception.
- Although you may intend having your children close together it is a good idea to give yourself a chance to recover

from one delivery before embarking on another pregnancy.

- Menstrual periods are very variable in women following delivery and especially for women who breastfeed. Some do not have a period until they stop breastfeeding completely; others have regular periods, some experience irregular bleeding throughout the time they feed their baby. Consequently, until you have re-established your cycle, natural methods of family planning may not be a reliable way of avoiding pregnancy.

- If you are breastfeeding you can take the progesterone only pill (known as the minipill). This is reliable but must be taken at about the same time each day to be most effective.

- If you are bottle-feeding you can take the combined pill (oestrogen and progesterone). However, some doctors prefer you to have at least one period after the birth before commencing the combined pill.

- Certain conditions during pregnancy can determine your options for contraception. For example, if you developed obstetric cholestasis (a condition caused by a hypersensitivity to oestrogen) during pregnancy, you will not be able to take the combined pill. Your GP will advise you accordingly.

- Some women choose to have a coil (intrauterine contraceptive device, or IUCD). This is a reliable form of contraception, which is easier and more comfortable to fit after you have had a baby, but can lead to heavier periods.

- If you used a 'cap' (diaphragm) prior to pregnancy, you will need to be refitted after childbirth. Do not be tempted to use your 'pre-baby' one again – it may not be reliable because you may need another size.

- When used properly, condoms are effective in preventing pregnancies, especially when accompanied by a spermicidal cream. As a couple, you may not favour them for long-term use, but if you want to wait a while before you decide on a more permanent method of contraception, they are very useful.

Keep an Eye on the Practicalities

Find Your Own 'Work-life Balance'
Decide what is most important to you and work towards making it the priority in your life. And don't forget, just because a certain choice of lifestyle suited a certain time, it doesn't necessarily mean that it will always be the case. Life moves on so keep reviewing things to make sure that you've still got the balance right.

Balance the Books
Keep an eye on your finances so that you don't suddenly find yourself facing unserviceable debt. If you suspect that you are not coping financially, seek help and do it sooner rather than later. Your local Citizens Advice Bureau is often a good place to start, or you might want to arrange a chat with your bank manager. Additionally, speak to your mortgage lender if you are concerned about paying your mortgage. Many of us have an in-built fear of people like bank managers but those who do make contact often discover that, rather than being two-headed monsters (apologies to any bank managers at this point), they really do want to help. Don't hide the brown envelopes and try to forget about the problem. The sooner you seek help, the sooner it will be sorted.

One mum has come up with a novel solution to her cash-flow problems. She keeps her credit card frozen in an ice block in her freezer. If she thinks about using it, she takes it out, knowing it takes 2-3 hours to thaw. This gives her just enough time to consider whether she really needs to make the purchase.

She swears it has saved her thousands of pounds in 'retail therapy' bills!

Make a Will

If you didn't do it before the arrival of your baby, you should seriously consider making a will – after all, it won't kill you! Many people don't fully appreciate the importance of planning for what would happen in the event of their death but having a written, signed will provides security for your child. You will need to think about appointing guardians and trustees for your child. One couple went as far as visiting the solicitor on the way home from the hospital following the birth of their first child, so strong was their motivation to get their affairs in order, just in case. Most people aren't quite so organised, but if you have thought about it before, but never done it, this could be the extra push you need.

 Top Tip: *Making a will is an important thing to consider – having one provides security for your family should anything happen to you.*

The End of the Beginning

So there you have it – the first six weeks. Hard work but brilliant and incredibly rewarding! Just a few weeks ago, you probably had difficulties getting your head around the idea that you would have a baby to look after, and now here you are doing it! And this is only the beginning – there's so much more to come! The good news, however, is that until you have to chase your teenage son or daughter around a football pitch, or race after your kids as they whizz around you on their bikes, most of it is far less physically demanding!

The first six weeks is a period of adjustment as you and your baby get to know each other and discover ways of coping with new parenthood. You probably feel your life has been temporarily turned upside down. Slowly but surely, however, things will pan out as you learn what does – and doesn't – work for your child. And final hints?

- Give yourself a bit of time to adjust and learn the basics – don't beat yourself up over mistakes.
- Make your child a priority and treasure the moments – babies grow incredibly quickly!
- Look after your partner – talk to them and listen to them. Share the load.
- Express your feelings. Be honest with those around you and don't suffer in silence.
- Look after yourself physically.
- Ask advice from others – no one expects you to have all the answers, all the time – but make your own decisions. Trust yourself.
- Accept offers of practical help.
- Get out with your baby and make friends.
- Try not to worry unnecessarily – work out today's priorities and deal with all that arises from them.
- Always ask professional advice if you're worried about your baby.
- Establish good habits now and keep going with them.
- Enjoy it! Build some fun – spontaneous and planned – into your life.

The Final Word

There is no such thing as the perfect mum and dad – we all make mistakes. But here is a great truth – your child needs you. He needs you desperately. Put bluntly, his relationship with you will be one of the most important in his life.

And one day, when he's grown up, your child will be asked, 'What was your mum or dad like?' His reply will encapsulate all your efforts as a mum or dad – beyond the first six weeks, beyond the first six years, maybe even beyond the first six decades. Now is the time to begin making sure that the answer he gives is one that you, and he, can be rightly proud of. Now is the first day of the rest of your life as a parent. So love your child, enjoy being with him and go for it!

Further Information

Organisations

Parentalk
PO Box 23142
London SE1 0ZT

Tel: 0700 2000 500
Fax: 020 7450 9060
e-mail: info@parentalk.co.uk
Web site: www.parentalk.co.uk

Provides a range of resources and services designed to inspire parents to enjoy parenthood.

Association for Postnatal Illness
145 Dawes Road
Fulham
London SW6 7EB

Tel: 020 7386 0868
Fax: 020 7386 8885
e-mail: info@apni.org
Web site: www.apni.org

Provides information, advice and support for women suffering from postnatal illness.

Baby Lifeline
Empathy Enterprise Building
Bramston Crescent
Tile Hill Lane
Tile Hill
Coventry CV4 9SW

Tel: 024 7642 2135
Fax: 024 7642 2136
e-mail: babyll@globalnet.co.uk
Web site: www.babylifeline.org.uk

Baby Lifeline is a national charity offering support to unborn babies, newborn babies and their mothers.

BLISS
2nd Floor
89 Albert Embankment
London SE1 7TP

Tel: 020 7820 9471
Fax: 0870 7700 3338

e-mail: info@bliss.org.uk
Web site: www.bliss.org.uk

Provides emotional and practical support to the families of babies who need intensive or special care.

Caesarean Support Network
55 Cooil Drive
Douglas
Isle of Man IN2 2HF

Tel: 01624 661269 (Mon–Fri, after 6 p.m., and weekends)

Offers emotional support and practical advice to mothers who have had or may need a Caesarean delivery.

Care for the Family
PO Box 488
Cardiff CF15 7YY

Tel: 029 2081 0800
Fax: 029 2081 4089
e-mail:
  care.for.the.family@cff.org.uk
Web site:
  www.care-for-the-family.org.uk

Provides support for families through seminars, resources and special projects.

Child Benefit Centre
Waterview Park
Pattenson Industrial Estate
Washington
Tyne and Wear NE38 8QA

Tel: 08701 555540

e-mail:
  childbenefit@mso4.dss.gov.uk
Web site: www.dss.gov.uk

Administers all child benefit claims.

The Child Psychotherapy Trust
Star House
104–108 Grafton Road
London NW5 4BD

Tel: 020 7284 1355
Fax: 020 7284 2755
e-mail: cp@globalnet.co.uk

Publishes useful leaflets for parents and other carers. Further details can be obtained by sending a SAE to the Trust at the above address.

Children 1st
41 Polwarth Terrace
Edinburgh EH11 1NU

Tel: 01313 378539
Fax: 01313 468284
e-mail: children1st@zetnet.co.uk

A national Scottish voluntary organisation providing advice and support to parents on the care and protection of their children.

Child Support Agency
In England:
PO Box 55
Brierley Hill
West Midlands DY5 1YL
Tel: 08457 133133

In Northern Ireland:
Great Northern Tower
17 Great Victoria Street
Belfast BT2 7AD
Tel: 028 9089 6896

The Government agency that assesses maintenance levels for parents who no longer live with their children.

Citizens' Advice Bureau (CAB)
Web site: www.nacab.org.uk

A free and confidential service giving information and advice on benefits, maternity rights, debt, housing, consumer, employment and legal problems as well as family and personal difficulties. Ask at your local library or look in your phone book for your nearest office.

Community Health Council
Look in the phone book for your local branch – they can tell you which GPs are working in your area and can put you in touch with your local health visitor

Contact-A-Family
209–211 City Road
London EC1V 1JN

Helpline: 0808 808 3555
Tel: 020 7608 8700
Fax: 020 7608 8701
e-mail: info@cafamily.org.uk
Web site: www.cafamily.org.uk

Brings together families whose children have disabilities.

Council for Disabled Children
8 Wakley Street
London EC1V 7QE

Tel: 020 7843 6061/6058
Fax: 020 7278 9512
e-mail: jkhan@ncb.org.uk
Web site: www.ncb.org.uk

Provides an information and advice service on all matters relating to disability for children and their families.

Couple Counselling Scotland
105 Hanover Street
Edinburgh EH2 1DJ

Tel: 0131 225 5006

Provides a confidential counselling service for relationship problems of any kind.

CRY-SIS (part of Serene)
BM CRY-SIS
London WC1N 3XX

Helpline: 020 7404 5011 (8 a.m.–11 p.m.)

Provides emotional support and practical advice to parents dealing with excessive crying, demanding behaviour and sleep problems.

Dads & Lads
YMCA England National Dads &
 Lads Project
Dee Bridge House
25–27 Lower Bridge Street
Chester CH1 1RS

Tel: 01244 403090
e-mail: dirk@parenting.ymca.org.uk
 ahowie@themail.co.uk

*Locally based projects run jointly by
YMCA and Care for the Family for
fathers and sons, mentors and boys.
They offer a unique opportunity to
get together with other fathers and
sons for a game of football and
other activities. To find out where
your nearest Dads & Lads project
is based or to get help starting a new
one, please contact Dirk Uitterdijk
at the above address.*

**Department of Social Security (now the
Department for Work and Pensions)**
In England:
Tel: 020 712 2171

In Northern Ireland:
Castle Buildings
Stormont Estate
Upper Newtownards Road
Belfast BT4 3SG
Tel: 028 9052 0500

National web site: www.dss.gov.uk

*Gives general advice on all social
security benefits, pensions and
National Insurance, including maternity benefits and income support.*

Disabled Parents' Network
Helpline: 0870 241 0450
e-mail: information@disabled
 parentsnetwork.org.uk
Web site: www.disabledparents
 network.org.uk

*A support network run by disabled
parents for disabled people thinking
about becoming parents, pregnant
disabled people and disabled
parents.*

Down's Syndrome Association
In England:
155 Mitcham Road
London SW17 9PG
Tel: 020 8682 4001 (Tues–Thurs
 10 a.m.–4 p.m.)

In Northern Ireland:
Graham House
Knockenbracken Healthcare Park
Saintfield Road
Belfast BT8 8BH
Tel: 028 9070 4606

In Wales:
206 Whitchurch Road
Cardiff CF14 3NB
Tel: 029 2052 2511

National web site:
 www.dsa-uk.com

Family Service Units
207 Old Marylebone Road
London NW1 5QP

Tel: 020 7402 5175
Fax: 020 7724 1829

e-mail: centraloffice@fsu.org.uk
Web site: www.fsu.org.uk

*Units across the country provide
support and advice for families with
problems.*

Fathers Direct
Tamarisk House
37 The Tele Village
Crickhowell
Powys NP8 1BP

Tel: 01873 810515
Web site: www.fathersdirect.com

An information resource for fathers.

The Foundation for the Study of Infant Deaths
14 Halkin Street
London SW1X 7DP

24-hour helpline: 020 7233 2090
Web site: www.sids.org.uk

*Provides cot death research and
support, including the Care of the
Next Infant (CONI) scheme for
parents who have lost a baby by
SIDS.*

Gingerbread
16–17 Clerkenwell Close
London EC1R 0AA

Tel: 020 7336 8183
Fax: 020 7336 8185
e-mail: office@gingerbread.org.uk
Web site: www.gingerbread.org.uk

*Provides day-to-day support and
practical help for lone parents.*

Health Development Agency
30 Great Peter Street
London SW1P 2HW

Publications: 01235 465565
Tel: 020 7222 5300
Fax: 020 7413 8900
Web site: www.hda-online.org.uk

*Produces a wide range of leaflets
and other useful information on a
variety of topics for families.*

Home-Start UK
In England:
2 Salisbury Road
Leicester LE1 7QR
Tel: 01162 339955
Fax: 01162 330232

In Northern Ireland:
133 Bloomfield Avenue
Belfast BT5
Tel/fax: 028 9046 0772

National e-mail address:
info@home-start.org.uk
National web site:
www.home-start.org.uk

*Volunteers offer support, friendship
and practical help to young families
in their own homes.*

La Lèche League of Great Britain
BM 3424
London WC1N 3XX

Tel: 020 7242 1278
Fax: 020 7831 9489
Web site: www.laleche.org.uk

Offers help with and information on breastfeeding. They can be contacted before or after the baby is born.

Maternity Alliance
45 Beech Street
London EC2P 2LX

Tel: 020 7588 8583
Fax: 020 7588 8584
e-mail:
  info@maternityalliance.org.uk
Web site:
  www.maternityalliance.org.uk

Works to improve rights and services for all pregnant women, new parents and their babies.

Meet-A-Mum Association (MAMA)
26 Avenue Road
London SE25 4DX

Helpline: 020 8768 0123 (Mon–Fri 7–10 p.m.)
Tel: 01761 433598
e-mail: meet-a-mum.assoc@blue yonder.co.uk
Web site: www.mama.org.uk

Provides counselling, practical support and group therapy for women suffering from postnatal depression.

Meningitis Trust
Fern House
Bath Road
Stroud
Gloucestershire GL5 3TJ

Tel: 0808 800 3344

Web site:
  www.meningitis-trust.org.uk

Supplies facts about meningitis and septicaemia and details of specific research.

Mind (National Association for Mental Health)
Granta House
15–19 Broadway
London E15 4BQ

Helpline: 020 8522 1278/0345 660 163 (Mon, Wed & Thur 9.15 a.m.–4.45 p.m.)
Tel: 020 8519 2122
Fax: 020 8522 1725
e-mail: contact@mind.org.uk
Web site: www.mind.org.uk

Has over 200 branches across England and Wales, most of which offer counselling services for individuals suffering from depression and other mental health problems. Mind's helpline offers advice and support.

National Association for Maternal and Child Welfare
40–42 Osnaburgh Street
London NW1 3ND

Tel: 020 7383 4117

Offers advice over the phone on childcare and family life.

National Association for People Abused in Childhood (NAPAC)
42 Curtain Road
London EC2A 3NH

NAPAC exists to assist adults who have experienced neglect or ill-treatment in childhood.

National Asthma Campaign
Providence House
Providence Place
London N1 0NT

Helpline: 0845 701 0203 (run by nurses 9 a.m.–7 p.m.)
Tel: 020 7266 2260
Web site: www.asthma.org.uk

The National Asthma Campaign is the independent UK charity working to conquer asthma, in partnership with people with asthma and all who share their concern, through a combination of research, education and support.

The National Autistic Society
393 City Road
London EC1V 1NG

Autism Helpline: 020 7903 3555 (Mon–Fri 10 a.m.–4 p.m.)
Parent to Parent: 0800 9520 520 (Your call is logged on an answer phone and the relevant regional volunteer calls you back)
Tel: 0870 600 8585
e-mail: autismhelpline@nas.org.uk
Web site: www.oneworld.org/autism-uk

National Childbirth Trust (NCT)
Alexandra House
Oldham Terrace
London W3 6NH

Breastfeeding line: 0870 444 8708
Tel: 0870 444 8707

Provides support for breastfeeding mothers as well as information on antenatal classes and postnatal groups.

National Childminding Association
8 Masons Hill
Bromley
Kent BR2 9EY

Advice line: 0800 169 4486 (Mon, Tues & Thurs 10 a.m.–12 & 2–4 p.m.; Fri 2–4 p.m.)
Tel: 020 8464 6164
Fax: 020 8290 6834
e-mail: info@ncma.org.uk
Web site: www.ncma.org.uk

Informs childminders, parents and employers about the best practice in childminding.

National Council for One Parent Families
255 Kentish Town Road
London NW5 2LX

Lone Parent Line: 0800 018 5026
Maintenance & Money Line: 020 7428 5424 (Mon & Fri 10.30 a.m.–1.30 p.m.; Wed 3–6 p.m.)
Web site: www.oneparentfamilies.org.uk

An information service for lone parents.

The National Eczema Society
Hill House
Highgate Hill
London N19 5NA

Information line: 0870 241 3604
  (weekdays 1–4 p.m.)
General enquiries: 020 7281 3553
Web site: www.eczema.org

The National Eczema Society is the only charity in the UK dedicated to providing support and information for people with eczema and their carers.

National Family and Parenting Institute
430 Highgate Studios
53–79 Highgate Road
London NW5 1TL

Tel: 020 7424 3460
Fax: 020 7485 3590
e-mail: info@nfpi.org
Web site: www.nfpi.org

An independent charity set up to provide a strong national focus on parenting and families in the twenty-first century.

National NEWPIN (New Parent and Infant Network)
Sutherland House
35 Sutherland Square
Walworth
London SE17 3EE

Tel: 020 7703 6326
Fax: 020 7701 2660
e-mail: quality@nationalnewpin.
  freeserve.co.uk

Web site: www.newpin.org.uk

A network of local centres offering a range of services for parents and children.

NHS Direct
Advice line: 0845 4647
Web site: www.nhsdirect.co.uk

NHS Smoking Quitline
Helpline: 0800 169 0169
Web site:
  www.giveupsmoking.co.uk

NIPPA (The early years organisation)
6C Wildflower Way
Belfast BT12 6TA

Tel: 028 9066 2825
Fax: 028 9038 1270
e-mail: mail@nippa.org
Web site: www.nippa.org

Promotes high-quality early childhood care and education services.

Northern Ireland Mother and Baby Action
Hope House
54 Scotch Quarter
Carrick Fergus BT38 7DP

Tel: 028 9332 9933
Fax: 028 9332 8967
e-mail: information@nimba.org.uk
Web site: www.nimba.org.uk

Provides support services for families who have experienced the birth of a baby that requires specialist care.

NSPCC
NSPCC National Centre
42 Curtain Road
London EC2A 3NH

Helpline: 0800 800 500
Tel: 020 7825 2500
Fax: 020 7825 2525
Web site: www.nspcc.org.uk

Aims to prevent child abuse and neglect in all its forms and give practical help to families with children at risk. The NSPCC also produces leaflets with information and advice on positive parenting – for these, call 020 7825 2500.

One Parent Families Scotland
13 Gayfield Square
Edinburgh EH1 3NX

Tel: 0131 556 3899/4563
Fax: 0131 557 9650
e-mail: opfs@gn.apc.org
Web site: www.gn.apc.org/opfs

Provides information, training, counselling and support to one-parent families throughout Scotland.

One Plus One
The Wells
7/15 Rosebery Avenue
London EC1R 4SP

Tel: 020 7841 3660
Fax: 020 7841 3670
e-mail: info@oneplusone.org.uk
Web site: www.oneplusone.org.uk

Aims to build, through research, a framework for understanding con-temporary marriage and partner-ship.

Parenting Education & Support Forum
Unit 431 Highgate Studios
53–79 Highgate Road
London NW5 1TL

Tel: 020 7284 8370
Fax: 020 7485 3587
e-mail: pesf@dial.pipex.com
Web site:
  www.parenting-forum.org.uk

Aims to raise awareness of the importance of parenting and its impact on all aspects of child development.

Parentline Plus
520 Highgate Studios
53–76 Highgate Road
Kentish Town
London NW5 1TL

Helpline: 0808 800 2222
Textphone: 0800 783 6783
Fax: 020 7284 5501
e-mail: centraloffice@parentline
  plus.org.uk
Web site:
  www.parentlineplus.org.uk

Provides a freephone helpline called Parentline and courses for parents via the Parent Network Service. Parentline Plus also includes the National Stepfamily Association. For all information, call the Parentline freephone number: 0808 800 2222.

Parents Advice Centre
Floor 4
Franklin House
12 Brunswick Street
Belfast BT2 7GE

Helpline: 028 9023 8800
e-mail: belfast@pachelp.org
Web site:
www.parentsadvicecentre.org

Parents Anonymous
6–9 Manor Gardens
London N7 6LA

Tel: 020 7263 8918 (Mon–Fri)

24-hour answering service for parents who feel they can't cope or feel they might abuse their children.

Parents at Work
45 Beech Street
London EC2Y 8AD

Tel: 020 7628 3565
Fax: 020 7628 3591
e-mail: info@parentsatwork.org.uk
Web site:
www.parentsatwork.org.uk

Provides advice and information about childcare provision.

Parents in Partnership – Parent Infant Network (PIPPIN)
49 Gordon Road
London E11 2RA

Tel: 020 8989 9056
Fax: 020 8989 9936
e-mail: martin@pippin.org.uk

Web site: www.pippin.org.uk

PIPPIN promotes the development of healthy parent and baby relationships in the period surrounding the birth.

Positive Parenting
1st Floor
2A South Street
Gosport PO12 1ES

Tel: 023 9252 8787
Fax: 023 9250 1111
e-mail: info@parenting.org.uk
Web site: www.parenting.org.uk

Aims to prepare people for the role of parenting by helping parents, those about to become parents and also those who lead parenting groups.

The Principal Registry of the Family Division
First Avenue House
42–49 High Holborn
London WC1V 6NP

Children section: 020 7947 6936
Web site: www.courtservice.gov.uk

Relate
In England:
Herbert Gray College
Little Church Street
Rugby CV21 3AP
Tel: 01788 573241

In Northern Ireland:
76 Dublin Road
Belfast BT2 7HP
Tel: 028 9032 3454

National e-mail address:
   enquiries@national.relate.org.uk
National web site:
   www.relate.org.uk

Provides a confidential counselling service for relationship problems of any kind. Local branches are listed in the phone book.

Stillbirth and Neonatal Death Society (SANDS)
28 Portland Place
London W1N 4DE

Helpline 020 7436 5881
Web site: www.uk-sands.org

Provides information and a national network of support groups for bereaved parents.

Twins and Multiple Birth Association (TAMBA)
Harnott House
309 Chester Road
Ellesmere Port
Cheshire CH66 1QQ

Helpline 01732 868000 (Mon–Fri 7–11 p.m.; weekends 10 a.m.– 11 p.m.)
Tel: 0870 121 4000
e-mail: enquiries@tambahq.org.uk
Web site: www.tamba.org.uk

Supplies information and support to families with twins, triplets and more.

Parenting Courses

- **Parentalk Parenting Course**
  A new parenting course designed to give parents the opportunity to share their experiences, learn from each other and discover some principles of parenting. For more information, phone 0700 2000 500.

- **Positive Parenting**
  Publishes a range of low-cost, easy-to-read, common-sense resource materials which provide help, information and advice. Responsible for running a range of parenting courses across the UK. For more information, phone 023 9252 8787.

- **Parent Network**
  For more information, call Parentline Plus on 0808 800 2222.

The **Paren**talk Parenting Course

Helping you to be a Better Parent

Being a parent is not easy. **Parentalk** is a new, video-led, parenting course designed to give groups of parents the opportunity to share their experiences, learn from each other and discover some principles of parenting. It is suitable for anyone who is a parent or is planning to become a parent.

The Parentalk Parenting Course features:

Steve Chalke – TV Presenter; author on parenting and family issues; father of four and **Parentalk** Chairman.
Rob Parsons – author of *The Sixty Minute Father* and *The Sixty Minute Mother*; and Executive Director of Care for the Family.
Dr Caroline Dickinson – inner city-based GP and specialist in obstetrics, gynaecology and paediatrics.
Kate Robbins – well-known actress and comedienne.

Each **Parentalk** session is packed with group activities and discussion starters.

Made up of eight sessions, the **Parentalk** Parenting Course is easy to use and includes everything you need to host a group of up to ten parents.

Each Parentalk Course Pack contains:
- A **Parentalk** video
- Extensive, easy-to-use, group leader's guide
- Ten copies of the full-colour course material for members
- Photocopiable sheets/OHP masters

Price £49.95

Additional participant materials are available so that the course can be run again and again.

To order your copy, or to find out more, please contact:

Parentalk
PO Box 23142, London SE1 0ZT
Tel: 0700 2000 500
Fax: 020 7450 9060
e-mail: info@parentalk.co.uk